Born in the Republic of Moldova in 1968, Gheorghe Virtosu has lived an intense and eventful life: after enjoying an idyllic childhood in his village, he left his parents' home at 15 for the middle school in town, which eventually led to a military career. Established in London in 1992, he gained British citizenship a few years later. Having simplicity as a guiding principle and solitude as his main source of inspiration, Gheorghe Virtosu is rapidly becoming a household name in literature, with his mammoth novel, *A Little Frog's Heart*, already a landmark on the compulsory reading list.

This volume is dedicated to one of my four sisters: Maria.

Gheorghe Virtosu

FAMILY LIFE – A BRIDGE BETWEEN HARMONY AND AGONY

Translation from Romanian: Mirela Bowen Hunt
Editor in Romanian: Adriana Nazarciuc
Illustrations by Diana Roscovan

AUSTIN MACAULEY PUBLISHERS™

LONDON * CAMBRIDGE * NEW YORK * SHARJAH

Ordering Information:
Quantity sales: special discounts are available on quantity purchases by corporations, associations, and others. For details, contact the publisher at the address below.

Publisher's Cataloging-in-Publication data
Virtosu, Gheorghe
Family Life – A Bridge Between Harmony and Agony

ISBN 9781643783260 (Paperback)
ISBN 9781643783277 (Hardback)
ISBN 9781645367468 (ePub e-book)

The main category of the book — Biography & Autobiography / Personal Memoirs

Library of Congress Control Number: 2019908138

www.austinmacauley.com/us

First Published (2019)
Austin Macauley Publishers LLC
40 Wall Street, 28th Floor
New York, NY 10005
USA

mail-usa@austinmacauley.com
+1 (646) 5125767

Maria was the joy, as much as she was the sorrow, of my childhood.

We used to belong to a large family, out of which Maria and I were the youngest of six siblings. She was three years older than me.

One by one, the older siblings left home and the village for the big schools in the city, each trying to find their path in life. Just like birds of a feather who desert the nest and spread their wings to fly the width and length of the earth. In the same way, all of them picked up and went off on their own personal quest to explore and discover their destiny in waiting. As human beings, we crave exhilaration and cradle the dream of self-fulfillment throughout our entire life, and my older siblings were no different in that respect.

During that time, Maria and I were still children in my parents' house and had years more to spend growing up together. Needless to say that Maria became my closest friend and ally in mischief, and I'm not counting for a moment the many occasions I got myself in trouble while ganging up with the other boys in the neighborhood.

Only Mom was closer to me at that time.

While the whole family lived under one roof, the age-gap between Maria and myself went unnoticed at the best of times, since everybody else regarded us as the youngest. As soon as we found ourselves the only children in the house, however, the fiercest rivalry broke out between us. And despite the relatively small difference in age, Maria used to play me for a fool all the time: being a girl stood in her favor, as she matured at a much faster pace and it soon became obvious that she had the upper-hand on me. I often looked at her and wondered whether I got my numbers right: how come that the three years separating us seemed more like ten? Perhaps many of the tactics she employed had been first-hand experience that she had to put up with while our older siblings were around. If so, it was only natural that she passed it down to me as you would with a set of clothes you've grown out of, but your youngest brother can still use.

Whatever the reason, Maria took every opportunity to trick me, making sure I took the entire blame for what was usually her own making. Even to this day, I think back and can't quite work out when and how the rivalry between us had turned utterly uncompromising and, at times, downright nasty.

Like all my other sisters, Maria was an eminent pupil in school from the beginning to the end. I, on the other hand, was trailing behind everybody else in my class. Odd situation to be in, which often had me puzzled as to why I had failed so badly where my sisters succeeded time and time again.

A possible answer to my question could be the teamwork which my sisters practiced all along amongst themselves. With Maria being the youngest of them, she had full attention most of the time, as the older ones were bending over backwards to please her.

Thus, having reaped the benefits of knowledge and wisdom from her senior siblings, Maria made it her mission in life to educate me in the same way she had been educated by our sisters. She had decided to keep me on the straight and narrow, and that was a promise to herself and to my parents!

Much as it suited me in principle, there was a very practical reason which faulted my sister's good intentions to elevate me: Maria has always been a bit of a tomboy. From very early on to present, she's exercised a rather strong will (otherwise known as pig-headedness) paired up with a hardliner manner of handling things. Had she been something else than a human, she'd make a great bullock! Or a great oak tree with healthy strong roots standing proud and tall, more willing to break than bend, if given the choice.

She was not anything you would expect in a gentle feminine nature which carries the resemblance of a whipping willow, flexing to and fro with the wind, sensitive to all its changes and moods. And just like in the case of a willow, a woman's greatest weakness becomes her greatest strength: the despondency to give in to love, the resilience in the face of great pain and sorrow, the incessant hope for the better and the tireless work to achieve it by skilfully combining intuition, belief, and unconditional support for their loved ones.

I've got to admit that in those early years Maria stood out for me as a particularly boisterous tomboy, whose bossy nature was only equaled by her intuition, which made her ten times more dangerous.

A born leader, without a doubt, Maria was but last in a long string of strong women in the family, very much like my mom and other sisters. Even so, Maria was in a class of her own. The inner strength she displayed stood on an equal footing with the strongest man's, any day. As siblings, we were all different, but similar: like the fingers of one hand which stem out of the same palm, but grow into different shapes and sizes. When called upon, we would all come together like the fingers of one hand scrunched up to make a fist, and in doing so we always had the acknowledgement that we were alike more than we were different: brothers and sisters of the same mother and father. This belief has stayed with me until this day.

Going back to my relationship with Maria, things went from bad to worse: despite her determination to make a brilliant student out of me, her patience would soon run short. As a more seasoned student, Maria knew the information backwards and every single time she tutored me she missed no opportunity to discipline me with a slap over the head at the slightest sign of distraction on my part.

But I wasn't one to stand for it, either. I thought of myself as an almost grown-up man who had already taken on a lot of responsibilities within the household: I single-handedly ran the maintenance and grooming of all the animals on the farm. She might have been my older sister, but that alone wouldn't give her the authority to treat me like dirt.

That would usually be the point at which all hell broke loose. Our poor cats would run for their lives trying to hide out of sight, bringing down pots and pans in their way, while the dog tied up at the back of the garden would take refuge in its kennel, in protest to our brotherly war. In other words, the cats and the dog in our household wouldn't hold each other sworn enemies the way we did!

As for my poor mom, I honestly don't know how she would put up with us during that time! We were at each other's throat all the time and the reason for it was often a silly one. I had decided in my mind that Maria wanted me trained as an obedient lap dog, and the thought of it made me wild with rage.

As time went by, our many quarrels and fights deepened the gap between us and we really got to the point where we couldn't see eye to eye over anything: if she said it was white, I would argue it was most definitely black, and the other way round! Thus, one thing led to another, and before I knew it, I was determined to make Maria's efforts to educate me go to waste just because I could! As you can easily imagine, Maria wouldn't take such defiance laying, and the both of us got caught up in a cycle of reprimand and retribution!

What frustrated me the most was Maria's ability to always be one step ahead of me, which I suppose came with the territory, since she was a girl and was older than me! Even so, I was never too far behind, forever watchful to seize my opportunity to catch her short. For instance, I remember she would storm out of the house even in bad weather with a cryptic look on her face which implied that a big secret which I couldn't know anything about was being carried out right under my nose. Then she would come back inside looking all serene and carefree as if to say that her ultra-secret confidential mission had been accomplished.

Her performance was enough to arise in me the greatest suspicion. In my turn, I'd rush out and start frantically searching for the proof that would reveal her big, dark secrets. Thus, with only that thought in my mind, I would go round and round in circles until I was frozen stiff. I needn't say that my investigations never came to anything; all Maria wanted to do was play mind games with me. It was her way of getting rid of me for a while and have the TV set all to herself, for that was another huge point of dissension between us. There was not much of a choice back in the olden days as we only had two channels broadcasting: one on current political issues, and the other one on educational topics. Apart from that, however, I think Maria took great pleasure in pulling my leg, and the instant gratification she would get out of it kept her happy for a while.

Revisiting that time of my life after so many years, I feel sorry for my mom who would get caught in the middle of our fights as she tried to make peace between us and to talk some sense in us:

"Dear me, dear me, much as I love you my precious babies, I wish you behaved more like a brother and a sister should to each other! People must be killing themselves laughing when they see you arguing and fighting over everything and anything!"

We sipped every word slipping off her lips, but no sooner had she finished, and we would start it all over again:

"Maria started it!"

"No, I haven't! He has!"

"Not true! It was her!"

"No, it was him!"

"If there was a place in this world where I could buy a grain of common sense, I'd be straight on my way!"

"Why would you want to buy a grain of common sense?" we asked her, bewildered.

We knew from dad that common sense was not something you could touch, smell or taste, let alone sell and buy! What did my mom mean by, 'a grain of common sense'?

"If I could get a grain of common sense, I'd split it evenly between the two of you in the hope that one day it would grow as big and strong as the acacia tree in our garden!"

"Do you mean to say that our minds are teeny-weeny?" I replied, suspecting that my mom thought we were a bit simple.

"What I mean is that your minds need to expand and become smarter, but also more understanding and tolerant towards each other and towards other people!"

I could tell even then that our misunderstandings were upsetting her greatly. All her efforts which summoned up years of parental experience would fall short of ever making a difference in the way the two of us treated each other.

To give you an idea of how wrong things used to go between Maria and I at the time, I remember my mom taking us fruit picking. To avoid the quarrels, she assigned each of us a tree at either side of her.

Little did she know that we would still take it out on each other, no matter what: getting stung by a buzzing bee, or having an overripe apple suddenly dropped on either one's head would be the other one's fault. That was enough to start a war then and there! Throwing fruit at each other, pulling faces, and calling names were among the strategies we often used. We carried on until one of us was hurt, yet the incident called for revenge and a hand-to-hand fight would begin! Poor Mom had to halt whatever she was doing and come running to pull us apart.

I am sure that a lot of people can relate to these sort of situations: you come across teasing, squabbling, and rough-playing in all families, but I think Maria and I took all of those to extreme and neither of us would give in!

As she was growing into a teenager, Maria had a lot of her friends coming around to our house when our parents were not at home. The girls would come together and do different things and I was not allowed to take part in any of it. Maria went to great lengths to keep me out of the picture by sending me around to a neighbor, a relative, or to do some imaginary task a long way away from home. After a while I wised up and even managed to beat them at their own game: I would go and come back very quickly, or simply refuse to go at all.

When they saw that the old tricks stopped working, they changed their strategy: they told me to go to the field over the other side of the hill, pretending Mom had sent for me. It was a long way to walk, especially for a young child, and the frustration doubled up when I reached the field only to find out that Mom had not called on me and had no idea what I was on about!

These tricks played at my expense contributed to flaring up my suspicion and my ill-feeling against Maria and her friends which cost me my peace of mind for a while. The more attempts to keep me away, the more determined I became to get to the bottom of whatever they were doing.

One day, Maria brought some friends home, as usual, and they found an excuse to send me away. Unlike the times when I would grumble and grouse, I agreed to it on the spot on this occasion; my lack of resistance took them aback and left them pleasantly surprised.

Still, they had their own agenda, and I had mine: I left the house, as if to go where they had sent me. Once out of sight, I took a sharp turn and came back on myself making sure that nobody caught a glimpse of me sneaking around! I took cover in a hide-out in my parents' garden and stood out, noticing everything going on around me.

What annoyed me the most was the fact that my own sister would rather do things with her friends than with her own brother. Hard as I tried, I could not get my head around it!

It wasn't long before I found out what they were up to that day: each girl had brought in an ingredient to make candy: some brought sugar, some walnuts, and others fetched plums. They heated up the pan and put in the ingredients, which, after a few minutes, began to give out the most inviting smell. I knew the candy they were making would turn out exactly like Grilliage, which were my favorite sweets. Of course, there was a lot of chit-chat as you would expect in any girls' party. My senses, however, were so wrapped up in the delicious flavor that all noise and chattering were blocked out. The suffering I went through that afternoon!

In the meantime, the girls started tucking in as soon as the first lot of candy came out of the pan. Avidly watching them eat from my hide-out, I felt my mouth watering and dribble involuntarily trickling down my chin.

Grilliage sweets were expensive to buy, and therefore, a rare treat. On seeing all those girls stuffing candy like there was no tomorrow, I couldn't help myself! Acting on impulse, I jumped out of my hide-out, ready to lecture the girls on how they shouldn't be selfish and share their candy with me. Looking back now, I can't think of a more naïve and ill-conceived plan, but hey, wisdom goes through the stomach especially when you are a little boy!

Without hesitation, Maria got hold of me and lifted me up by the ears, while other girls slapped me on the back of my neck so hard that I could see yellow sparks in front of my eyes.

"You little liar!" Maria scolded me. "Why am I even surprised to find you sneaking on us! That's exactly what a good-for-nothing like you would do!" she carried on, telling me off in front of the other girls, to my great shame. "You must swear on your life that you won't tell anyone about this! Go on! Do it!" she cornered me, keeping hold of my ear as tight as ever.

While the girls were ganging up on me, a whole lot of questions kept swarming through my mind: why was candy-making such a big secret that no one could find out about? Why would they want to swear me to secrecy about it? As far as I could tell, they had done a wonderful job working as a team. My only problem was that they refused to share the candy with me!

Just to get them off my back, I did what they asked me. They ended up the hullabaloo with a few more slaps on different sensitive parts on my body and then let me go, assuming I had paid fairly for my indiscretion. But I had other thoughts! How did they ever think they were going to get away with it: they were the guests and I was technically the host, to add insult to injury, I had to face up to the fact that I had just had my ears bashed in by a bunch of girls! My blood was boiling, and my hurt pride cried out for revenge!

I headed to the shed where my dad kept his working tools and looked for something suitable. I grabbed the spade and balanced it in my hands for a few seconds, before I shoved it to the side. I looked for the scythe, but, fortunately, couldn't reach it. I say fortunately because who knows what tragedy might have come of it in those moments of blind fury. All I could think about at the time was the huge humiliation I had been subjected to in my own house by a bunch of girls!

Eventually, I picked up a fork which I was quite familiar with. Light-weight and easy to handle, it seemed like the perfect choice for carrying out my plan. I was going to teach these girls a lesson which they would always remember! Waving the fork like a weapon of war, I stormed out of the shed blasting out my cry of revenge:

"I'll show you who the landlord is in this household, you spoilt brats!"

The girls took a glance at me and another at Maria who urged them:

"Run for your lives, girls!"

Panic-stricken, the girls scattered all around trying to confuse me. They even threw candy at me to buy themselves some time and get as far away from me as possible. But my craving for candy had gone and a wish to reinstate my honor, which laid in tatters, replaced it.

What a sight they were as they were running around in circles like a herd of frightened does! Each of them aimed for the gate, but none of them could work out how to unlock it as they were climbing over one another in their hasty attempt to escape me. In the end, the nimbler ones began jumping over the gate and the others followed them quickly, except for this little girl, Larisa Prepelita. She was a plump girl, a couple of years older than me. She stopped in front of the locked gate at a loss as to what to do next, pleading to her friends who were already on the other side:

"Girls, please help me out of here!" she implored stomping her feet as if that would have helped her take off the ground. "Don't leave me behind with the wilder beast, please!" she screamed in terror while I was getting closer and closer to her.

My crimson-red face with googly eyes and a grizzly grin would have been enough to scare off anyone: the dog had taken shelter at the back of the kennel, and the little girl's cry for help had been muffled out by the hysterical screams of the others. Larisa lost her cool and was stumbling over her feet like a headless chicken trying to move around the place and back to the gate. She didn't know how to unlock the gate and that added to her panic.

Blinded by my anger, I launched the fork in her direction determined to take my revenge. Thank goodness she ducked out of the way, while the fork became firmly stuck in the right hand-side gatepost. In a moment of clarity, as she realized what a narrow escape she had, the girl started shrieking and screaming in fear of her life.

Echoing her horror, the other girls let out a wail; their shouting and screaming ominously resembled a wailing sound, as they were in no doubt that something bad had happened to Larisa.

As for Larisa, she charged at the gate, used the fork as a step to give herself a boost and over the gate she flew head-first. She landed awkwardly on the other side, hurting her ankle and head, but she wasted no time pondering over minor injuries. She picked herself up and limping as fast as she could, headed off in the direction where the other girls had gone. She was screaming at the top of her lungs, numbed by the shock of the near-death experience she had just gone through!

Now that I think of it, I couldn't be more grateful for missing that little girl that day, for otherwise my temporary folly would have come to a great tragedy.

Anyway, that was the end of it on that occasion with all the girls just about managing to get away safe and sound. As usual, Maria was the focus of my revenge and her friends but collateral damage in the fight between us.

With the girls out of the way and the peace and quiet precariously restored within our household, I went to the gate trying to dislodge the fork from where I had stuck it. It took me a while to do so which gave me a bit of time for reflection. By the end of it, I was secretly thankful for Larisa's good reflexes which saved her life and saved me from ruining mine. Although of a young age, the realization of what could have happened made me aware of the dangers of bad temper.

To top up my triumph, I opened the gate and got out into the street shouting at the girls like a little puppy who wouldn't go far from home for he knows he can bark the loudest in his own courtyard:

"I swear I'll pull your hair out if any of you sets foot again in this courtyard!"

Going back into the courtyard, I found the scythe which must have fallen out the back of my bike when I had returned home from the field earlier, with bags full of fresh grass for chickens. I was glad to have it back as I had thought it was lost. I quickly grabbed it and started pompously waving it in the direction of the girls who were out of reach, but still in sight. I could tell they were all panting heavily, partly because of the run, and partly because of the nasty shock I had given them. They gathered around Maria, comforting and pitying one another.

"As for you, sis, looking forward to seeing you back home. I've even got a present for you: the nose ring which belonged to the bullock taken to the slaughter-house last year. The two of you share the same sort of temper, you know!"

I went back inside with my chest puffed up. I kind of knew that it wasn't much to be proud of in what I had done to the girls, but my childish pride pushed me to act all cocky. I took one look at the dog who was edging out of the kennel, not entirely sure whether it was safe to do so. His tail timidly waging from side to side as if to reassure me of his loyalty.

"Don't worry, boy," I encouraged him, "you have nothing to do with this mess! I'm counting on your help with it, you know!"

I summoned all the strength I was capable of and finally got the fork unstuck. I tided away both the fork and the scythe and then I went to pick up all the candy the girls had thrown at me. The chickens had a taste of it, but soon lost interest and pooped all over it. Rather resentful at their reaction, I picked up all the candy in a bucket and gave it to the pigs who were happy to have it. No wonder chickens have a reputation for being little-brained!

I did all the washing-up and cleaning in the kitchen and left everything spotless, so Mom wouldn't become suspicious. After all, the girls had my word that I wasn't going to grass them up and I had no intention of going back on my promise, although I couldn't help being bemused at the shroud of secrecy which surrounded the whole thing: why would a session of confectionary suddenly turn into a forbidden thing? We had cooking classes in school and nobody argued with it!?

To me, the greatest upset on the day was their selfish attitude and the refusal to share with me the goodies. Years later, when I asked Maria why they were hiding from our parents the confectionary-making, she couldn't give me a good reason for it. Silly, really!

After tidying up in the kitchen, I gathered whatever had been left behind by the girls and was still edible and sat myself down on the porch, enjoying every bite.

The sweetness of the candy washed away any trace of grudge against the girls: they had done a wonderful job! The candy made up for all my heartache and I knew in my heart that I had forgiven them!

Later on in the evening, when I heard the gate screech, I ran out to see Mom and Maria coming through. My sister realized she had gone a step too far that time and didn't dare show up on her own to face me, so she had waited for Mom to return from the field.

I stood on the porch, pulling the most innocent face.

"There you are, Gheorghita!" my mom greeted me in a gentle voice.

"Here I am, Mom!" I answered back, avoiding looking Maria in the eyes.

"Have you fetched some fresh grass to feed the animals?" she wanted to know as usual.

"I have," I replied half-heartedly.

Mom stared at me questioningly and then moved her attention to Maria. She could tell something was up between us (again!!!), but in the absence of a give-away, no blame would be laid on anyone! The lack of arguments and quarrels was not necessarily a good sign: the unusual peace and quiet together with my determination to stay on task with the jobs in the household looked too good to be true...

Mom gaped at the sky above, fishing for an answer: could it be that her prayers were finally answered by God and the quarrels had been replaced by goodwill and understanding between the two of us?

Sly like a fox, Maria seized the moment when Mom was not paying attention and quickly nipped to the kitchen. She saw at a glance that the place had been cleaned and tided up. Reassured, she turned on her heels and let Mom know as she passed us:

"I'll be inside doing my homework, Mom!"

She took a furtive glimpse at me and prompted me to wipe the caramel from around my mouth. I did so, as we were both united in our wish to hide from Mom what had happened earlier that day.

"I don't know what the two of you are cooking up, but I hope none of it is mischief! Anyway, let's get back to whatever needs doing around here..." she concluded carrying her working bag inside the kitchen.

Schoolwork was something Mom would never interfere with, and when it came to my sisters, Mom was religious about allowing them the time and space for doing homework. She lived precariously through her daughters and she loved to see them progressing and getting good marks, hoping there was a good future in store for them.

Eventually, the day came to an uneventful end and we put our grudges aside for a while, until next time when we found a reason for fight and disgruntlement. I would only say that every time the war was on, all the past discontent resurfaced and came back to life like a restless ghost! Each of us felt obliged to outdo the other, fueling a never-ending cycle of fight and friction.

Speaking of which, another one of Maria's pranks comes to mind. It was one of those days in spring when sunshine and tree blossom mixed up in the air and gave out a fresh sweet fragrance. More importantly, we were celebrating St George's Day, which really brought it home to me: St George being my personal patron, I was looking forward for the day every year as I would get lots of presents and undivided attention. That year was no exception: showered with attention and gifts according to the custom, I felt like the lord of the castle. The high spirits took me away for a while from the mundane conflicts my sister and I had ongoing.

But just as I let my guard down, Maria was there waiting for her opportunity to play her tricks on me.

"Gheorghita, hey, Gheorghita!" she called in a mellow voice. "I'm keeping a humongous secret which I have to share with you, otherwise I'll burst like an overripe tomato!"

Everything, from the frown in her brow to the secretive tone in her voice, held the promise of mystery and adventure. My sister knew me well: if there was anything I couldn't quite resist, that was a hidden secret waiting to be revealed! I used to think of myself as a mastermind able to decipher codes and read situations! I was so convinced of it, that it never crossed my mind that it might have been all in my head!

"What secret are you talking about?" I asked trembling with anticipation.

Maria was a born actress and when she wanted, she would put to work a full range of abilities. On those occasions, her normal self which was patronizing and rather dismissive of me, turned into a persuasive and engaging personality. My sister's transformation from tormentor into partner in crime appealed to me on so many levels! Sharing her secret and having her as an ally at the same time was a dream come true!

"What's the secret?" I asked lowering my voice for fear I could dispel the mystery in case somebody else overheard me.

"Come with me!" Maria urged me in the same tone, peeking all around to make sure that no one eavesdropped, not even the birds in the sky.

We hid in the garden, away from everybody else's eyes.

"Wait here!" Maria instructed me, sensing she had the upper-hand. Totally under her spell, I soaked in every gesture she made, and she surely didn't hold back: to give it a sense of drama, Maria walked to the garden gate and stuck her head over the fence looking left, right, and middle for spies. By that point, I was convinced my sister would share with me her greatest and darkest secret which would put me in charge of her destiny. I imagined how I could blackmail her by threatening to tell everybody, and thus finally break her spirit and her hold on me. Never did it cross my mind that Maria was doing exactly that to me!

She tip-toed in my direction pursing her lips as if to let me into her secret, but just then the clanging of the dog's chain stopped her in her tracks. She frowned, swiftly turned on her heels and darted off to settle the dog. I couldn't help but sneak to the corner of the house to have a little peek. Maria was taking extra measures to ensure her secret stayed only between the two of us: she leant over the gate in case uninvited company tried to pry.

I was dying to find out! My mind raved on like the engine of a powerful car stuck into overdrive. My eyes goggling out of my head and my mouth slack, I must have been a right sight to Maria! Whatever that secret was, I couldn't be readier for it!

"Gheorghita, there is something else we need to do first…" she announced whisperingly.

"What else do we need to do?" I fretted, taken aback by yet another delay.

"You'll have to swear that you won't tell anyone about the secret!"

"Of course, I won't tell anyone! That's why it's called a secret!" I tried to wiggle my way out of it.

"No, no, no! You'll have to swear by it!" she shook her head to let me know that she wouldn't have it any other way.

"Right… OK… I'll swear…" I muttered.

"That's more like it!" she cheered up. "You'll have to swear…" she paused, completely aware I was hanging on her every word, "on the beauty spot on your right cheek!" she delivered the blow quickly and painfully.

The beauty spot on my right cheek Maria was talking about was my pride and joy, especially after listening to one of Mom's stories recounted on a full moon night just before we went to bed. Maria and everybody else in the family had a pretty good idea how fond I was of my beauty spot. It was the first thing I'd check out when I stared in the mirror at myself. It was the peculiarity which made me special and unique. But my great strength proved to be my great weakness, and Maria, sly as usual, had banked on it.

I expected anything but that! Maria's words echoed in my ears for a while before the meaning traveled all the way down to my brain. She had me dumbstruck.

"What you've got to remember here, Gheorghita, is that I'm letting you into a great mystery…"

"I got that!" I mumbled grumpily. "You keep saying that!"

"I found out about it from…" she started in a shaky voice which perfectly balanced anticipation and uncertainty.

"Go on, who did you find it out from?" I urged choking with curiosity.

"From…" she prolonged my agony, planning each pause carefully.

"Well, from Auntie Vera…" she burst out in the end.

"When?!" I continued demanding answers.

"Yesterday in the afternoon!"

"Which Auntie Vera are you talking about, now!?" I carried on shooting one question after another as I was trying to reassure myself that it was a genuine secret, but against my best instinct, I felt myself slipping deeper and deeper in the web of illusion Maria was weaving around me.

"What do you mean which Auntie Vera?!" Maria skilfully avoided the answer implying I was a bit of a dimwit, which restored her control over the whole situation. She pulled an offended face, stepped back and stared at me half mockingly, and half pityingly. By that she wanted to point out how lucky I was to be me and become part of such a big conspiracy.

"Auntie Vera, our next-door neighbor, you silly sausage," she filled me in, acting annoyed I made her waste time with such unimportant details.

"You mean the one whose house is behind ours?" I didn't want to give in.

"Yeah, that one…" she finally conceded as she shifted her attention to scrutinizing the road up and down for some undercover spies.

"And stop saying names out loud, will you?!" she scolded, slapping the back of my head. My head bent forward under her nudge and my eyes rested on a swarm of tiny bugs which were busying themselves, running around my feet. For a moment, I thought they had tumbled off the crown of my head when my sister slapped me. I checked them out with suspicious eyes. My sister had me thinking that even those puny creatures could jeopardize our secret. She was a master of mind games, especially when it came to tricking me!

"I happened to be there when Auntie Vera said…" Maria started spinning it out.

"You happened to be there!?" I repeated mesmerized with a tinge of distrust in my voice.

"That's right, I went around to see Grandma Gafia, her good neighbor and friend," Maria used a stern tone as if to put me in my place for doubting her.

"OK, OK, get on with it! What did she say?" I whispered my words gasping with excitement since rumors had it that Auntie Vera was the village witch.

In fact, that bit of information had everything to do with Maria, yet again! One evening when she was getting ready to go out with her friends, Maria took me to the side to warn me about Auntie Vera's witchcraft, letting me know in great confidence that she was particularly keen on getting her hands on little children like me, whose flesh was sweet and tender. You can tell my sister didn't do things by half, and fear has a quick ear: for a long time afterwards, I remember being terrified to go out after dark. This way, my sister kept me at bay for a while, until I was old and wise enough to realize her bluff.

I admit that her stories about Auntie Vera gave me nightmares over many nights.

"Auntie Vera is a powerful and dangerous witch who turns into a young maiden at night and wanders around on the back of a horned donkey. The donkey itself is a servant of the evil forces which reign supreme around the deserted monasteries where devils and demons come to party all night!"

She would embellish her horror stories with all kinds of ludicrous details, never forgetting to drop hints of what I was expected to do (or not do!). She had me promise I would never get out at night because Auntie Vera would kidnap all the naughty little children who didn't listen to and get on well with their older sisters (remind you of someone?). Before I knew it, Maria had turned me into her little lap dog.

Thus, on that occasion when Auntie Vera's name came up in conversation, I swallowed hard and felt a shiver slide down my spine, which did not go unnoticed with Maria:

"You see, Gheorghita, that's why you ought to swear on your beauty spot that you'll guard the secret with your life! If anyone finds out about it, we'll both be in mortal danger!"

"I swear on my beauty spot!" I slurred my words, terrified, but as starved for secrets as ever.

"This means you can't tell Mom or Dad about it, even if we have our greatest fall out ever!" she pointed her finger at me.

By the way she acted, Maria drove me up the wall and I could feel my emotions run high. Deep down I was determined not to say a word to anyone, but the increased pressure of my vow made me want to spill the beans then and there!

"I swear! I swear!" I kept chanting at the end of my wits. "Just get on with it, Maria!"

By that stage, Maria must have been very proud of herself as she had achieved and exceeded what she had set out to do.

"All right, all right, I believe you'll stand by your word. Besides, if you are not man enough to do that, what good are you?" she couldn't help digging her claws even deeper in my tattered pride.

"For goodness sake, just tell me what it is!" I burst out impatiently.

"Even your closest friends can't know about it!" she stuck to her guns relentlessly.

"Of course not! I've just given you my word!"

I was so worked up that I could have cried a river! Without any warnings, Maria reached out and grabbed me by the ear. The pain made me pull back and get into a fighting position.

"Steady, boy," Maria patronized me. "I was only trying to catch a mosquito which was resting on your ear!"

I made an effort to calm myself down, but Maria wouldn't stop there: in a flash, she stooped over me and plucked out a hair.

"You should thank me for getting that flea for you! You must have picked it up while playing with the dog… Oh bother, I've lost it now!" she smirked.

I looked at her in disbelief but did not dare contradict her. She was again toying with my fears: I had a real dislike for fleas and all the trouble they brought with them.

"But coming back to our business… I was only able to pick up on this totally by accident… well, there was a bit of eavesdropping on my part…"

In an instant, I would forget about mosquitoes and fleas, and start gawping at her, desperate for the final revelation. What a delightful picture that must have been for Maria! I used to be such a gullible little boy!

"Just spit it out, Maria, will you?" I implored with tears in my eyes.

"I heard Auntie Vera saying…" she whispered.

"Who was she saying it to?" I asked hurriedly hoping to speed up the pace of the conversation.

"To some women, who else!" she posed offended by the many interruptions I was causing.

"Who were the women?" I carried on questioning, eager to learn who Auntie Vera's accomplices were to stay out of their way. Maria's stories about the witch who kidnapped children and mummified them were giving me sleepless nights.

"I have no idea; I couldn't exactly stick my head over the fence to have a good look at them!" Maria tormented me.

"What time of the day was it? Evening, late at night, midnight perhaps…" I would frantically inquire.

"Let me think… It was late evening, after sundown…"

"Yes, go on!" I urged.

"As you know, Auntie Vera's fence is lined up with all these tall beanstalks which stop prying eyes from seeing anything…"

"I know…" I nodded at her.

"Well, here is something you don't know: at night all these beanstalks turn into humongous thorn bushes so that uninvited guests who creep around the place get impaled and die a terrible death!"

Maria borrowed the horror imagery from our immediate reality: we had lots of thorn bushes growing wild in the moorlands and the picture she was describing was compatible with it.

"You've seen the poor birds which get entangled and struggle until they die in the thorns… It's the same with the unfortunate people who happen to be around Auntie Vera's cottage after dark. I've told you before about it… Demons come and go as they like, guided around the place by owls and bats, and many naughty children found their end in Auntie Vera's midnight supper, thus helping her to stay young and beautiful forever and ever…"

"Yeah, yeah, you've already told me about all of that!" I rushed her, unwilling to refresh my memory on the sordid details. I had spent many nights buried under my duvet with that terrifying stuff playing in my mind over and over again; the last thing I needed was Maria taking me through it all again.

"So, you remember all the stories, that's good!" she wouldn't let it go that easily.

"Get to the point, Maria! What's the secret?"

"The secret, of course, that's why we are here!" she babbled on. "Well, here is the secret if you want to know: I overheard Auntie Vera saying something about St George's Day… Something to do with those celebrating St George as their patron…"

"That's me, I've been celebrating St George's Day today because he is my patron..." I started murmuring. 'I understand now: she is sharing the secret with me in the hope that she'll be able to partake in the privilege of seeing her own wishes come true, like me...' I thought to myself.

St George's Day had always been extra-special for me: it was like a third birthday in the year. According to my mom, my official birthday on the 17th of April had, in fact, been wrongly registered, as my real coming into the world happened on the 14th of April. Apart from those days, however, St George's Day was always full of fun and surprises and that year my mom had gifted me with a very smart shirt early in the morning, while everybody else made a fuss of me. We all ate good food, spent time together, and enjoyed ourselves greatly.

I purposely blinked a few times to make myself reconnect with the present moment. It was becoming clearer that Maria had loaded the whole situation in her favor!

"Are you still following me, Gheorghita?" she demanded my attention, sensing me slipping away. "Auntie Vera spoke for a long time to her fellow witches that night, and all the crows in the trees took to their wings and made the sky go even darker. They either wanted to find out for themselves what the witches were up to, or maybe they were just providing them with cover and distraction against spies... And the noise they were making... you should have been there... it was nothing like their ordinary cawing..."

In our neighborhood the cawing of the crows made a consistent wall of sound we all grew familiar with in time.

"Are you listening to me?" Maria grabbed my shoulders and started shaking me.

"I am, I am..." I assured her in a jolted voice.

"Vroom, vroom, vrooooom... they were riding their brooms around the place." Maria imitated the witches.

My sister carried on her imaginary flight on a broom for a while, just enough to annoy me.

"They said that on St George's Day at sundown..." she went on.

Maria looked around again feigning caution, and I did the same, imitating her every move like a little well-trained monkey.

"You know the pear tree at the bottom of our garden, don't you?" she unexpectedly changed the topic.

"What pear tree?" I replied blinking fast and furious in bafflement.

"The pear tree which makes the sweet juicy pears we so much like..."

"Of course, I know which one... What about it?"

"Very well, now... Auntie Vera said that if someone called George went around such a tree ten times on St George's Day..."

"Yes, went around ten times on St George's Day…" I echoed her words like a parrot, shuffling towards her for fear that I might miss something.

"… while keeping a hand on the trunk of the tree for this way the link between heavens and the earth is activated and all your wishes will come true! Your wishes will go straight to God and be granted!"

"Let me get this right!" I interrupted pulling myself even closer to her.

"I haven't finished yet!" Maria scolded me.

"Fair enough…" I conceded. "Carry on!" I urged her breaking up in goose bumps all over my body.

"Every time you go around, the pear tree will get you a granted wish…" Maria clarified it for me.

"Which means that for ten wishes…" the penny finally dropped with me.

"For ten wishes you've got to go ten times around the tree," Maria put me straight.

"Go around the tree you say, hey! It makes sense… I had a dream last night…" I interrupted.

"A dream! What did you dream?" Maria couldn't resist asking.

"I dreamt a white eagle…" I muttered.

"An angel!" Maria burst out wisely. "Probably St George himself!" she concluded.

"No, no, it wasn't an angel or St George, it was a white eagle," I dared to contradict her.

"Whatever you say, Gheorghita!" she accepted. "No matter how you look at it, it's definitely a sign that something extraordinary is going to happen to you," she announced in a rather serious tone, as she flapped her arms while going around in circles to imitate the flight of the eagle. Her great talent of putting a twist on everything to suit her purpose paid off every single time: she took what I told her and used it against me.

The worst thing was that I would fall for it without fail: by that stage, I was convinced that a miracle was taking place and I was at the center of it all!

"Every time you go around the tree, you'll have to speak out loud a wish," Maria carried on making up the rules. "But remember: you'll have to keep the palm of your hand on the trunk of the tree and not cease contact for one moment, otherwise the link will be broken and the fulfilment of your wishes will not find its way back to you!" Maria warned me in a doom-and-gloom voice.

"You mean this is a bit like an electric shock," I tried to make sense of it. "Remember when I touched the TV set and got electrocuted? Lucky I could pull myself away quickly!" The unpleasant memory dulled a bit the warm glow of expectation which had been nestling in my chest for a while.

"Something like that!" Maria agreed.

I felt dumbstruck with mixed emotions; big eyes, mouth wide open, ideas spinning around in my head at a dizzying speed.

"Don't you believe me, Gheorghita?" Maria misinterpreted my state of prostration.

"I believe you…" I whispered back, almost choking at the enormous potential which had just opened up in front of me.

I had always been full of big ideas, great expectations, and ardent wishes, but all of those things seemed to suddenly vanish away when faced with the prospect of coming true in the blink of an eye. I had trouble grasping even those wishes I used to fantasize all the time about.

I used to envy the young boys and girls who were the subject of wish-making superstitions at certain times of the year, and I secretly wished the years of my life passed on faster to be like them. I knew, for instance, about the custom of tying the gates of the houses where young, desirable girls lived on St Andrew's Day. On the same day young girls would write down on a piece of paper their wishes and burn it at dusk as they tried to decipher the future in the play of the shadows on the walls. I recall all those occasions when I would hide away and watch it all, so afraid of being discovered and thrown out, that I wouldn't even breathe. I remember the girls secretly whispering amongst themselves things which I couldn't hear, filling up the gaps with my own thoughts, wishes, and fanciful ideas.

Maria would take full advantage of my trusting nature and had me eating from the palm of her hand. She would tell me little lies and made-up superstitions which I believed without questioning. Thus, the news of such a brilliant wish-fulfilling practice made me happy beyond belief!

In the meantime, Maria who was scrutinizing me, fell short of guessing what was on my mind and finally cracked:

"What are you thinking about?" she wanted to know. But my mind was somewhere else and didn't register she was talking to me.

"Gheorghita!" she screamed in my ear which made me jump. "What are you thinking about?"

"Nothing, it's nothing!" I quickly retorted.

"Don't even think of pulling a fast one on me!" she warned me.

"It never crossed my mind, anyway… Why would you think that?" I defended myself.

"I've just told you the biggest of secrets and look what I get in return…" she said in a strop.

But I couldn't care less of Maria and her moods: I had found out a wondrous secret and was determined not to share it with anyone since I had sworn on my beauty spot to keep it. As far as I was concerned, Maria could go and throw her tantrums somewhere else!

"Honestly, Maria, I'm not thinking of anything of the kind…"

"How do you expect me to believe that when I'm talking to you and you can't even be bothered to reply. You look through me, it's like you're far away and I'm not here…" she said reproachfully, waving an arm in front of my face, trying to make out that she could have been invisible for all I cared.

"I'm far away and you're not here… What kind of nonsense is this, Maria? I'm here and so are you!"

"You silly boy!" she retorted. "What I meant was that you are distracted!" she explained pressing her thumb against my forehead so hard that it hurt. Then, with a quick twist of the wrist, she plucked another one of my hairs out. "You're welcome, I've just gotten rid of another flea for you!" she mocked me just as I was about to retaliate.

Despite the sharp pain, I chose not to react to her nasty practical joke. All I could think about was the good fortune waiting for me at the end of the day. But Maria wouldn't have me ignoring her, no way!

"I knew you were going to get cold feet after sharing with you the secret…" she tried to wind me up. I said nothing to that, so she continued in a high-pitch voice.

"Yes, sir, I could tell you would go sour on me!" she moaned. "You've been after that secret all along and now that you know everything, chuck poor Maria to the side and tell her nothing! Typical of a little selfish boy like you!" she pretended to go away in a huff.

I for one, however, was really and truly lost for words. Oblivious at the world around, I sat there focusing all my strength on the inner struggle. I was battling my own thoughts, trying to discern amongst them and pin down my greatest wishes.

My little brain had, all of a sudden, become the playground where wishful thinking was playing at hide-and-seek with Maria's whimsical words about witchcraft and wish-fulfilling magic. All I had to do was decide upon which one would be first, which one last and everything in between!

"I'll make my way to the pear tree as soon as the sun has gone down…"

It was the only pear tree of its kind in our garden: the Motrin Pear tree. The fruit it used to bear drew me like a magnet to it during the harvest season: big plump pears, golden and juicy, heavenly sweet. If love had a taste, that must have been it!

Since we were only halfway through springtime, the pear had no fruit on it yet. But my newly acquired knowledge of its special powers gave it a magical glow. But I wasn't that naïve to think that I could be the only one in the know of it; surely my sisters, especially Maria would have sought to take advantage of it, too. I might have been at the front of the queue because I carried the same name as St George, but I could just imagine Maria following closely, stumbling over her own feet as she hurried round and round the pear tree to get her wishes to come true. With that image in mind, I pondered over whether I should go first to make sure that the wish-fulfilling powers of the pear tree hadn't been wasted all on Maria's desires, or should I wait to see her performing the ritual and learn how to go about it good and proper? Besides, if I went second, I would have found out what Maria's greatest wishes were. That looked like a prime opportunity for it, considering that Maria rarely, if ever, opened up to me! Tough choice!

In the meantime, at the back of my mind, my wishlist started to take form, although I had trouble prioritizing: no sooner had I decided upon a wish, another one would come to mind claiming a place on my list!

There was something, however, which had to be first on my wishlist and I wouldn't have had it any other way: it was about one of my sisters, Nadia. Nadia had always been quite frail and sickly. Her nose would bleed often and for no obvious reason, which was why she would spend a lot of time resting in bed while doctors would pay visits at home. During the check-ups, Mom would get us all out of the house and kept private counsel with the doctor as to what needed to be done about my sister's condition. Needless to say, that the privacy of it all increased our curiosity.

As a child growing up in my parents' house, I remember the constant worry which hovered over our household like a dark cloud. My parents tried everything; they even took Nadia to Ukraine, to a seaside resort called Sergeevka. None of the doctors who saw my sister could give a diagnosis, but they had all agreed that sea air might benefit her.

Therefore, my greatest wish of all and the first on my list was that Nadia would get well and never have a nosebleed again!

All that faith I had placed on the revelation that Maria had opened my eyes to, filled me to the brim and exulted through all my pores. It was St George's Day, the only day in the year when I could get the job done and I intended doing so without delay.

After our secret discussion which took place around lunch-time, I couldn't wait until the end of the day. I was fussing around, frolicking here and there and everywhere, wishing time had galloped by and night had fallen sooner on the day. Ever since I was a child, I couldn't bear waiting for things to happen; for me that was a killer. The only way I could take the passing of time kindly was to occupy myself with something. I decided to keep myself busy by going out to the field to fetch some food for the animals. I quickly got on my bike and rode it as fast as I could. The effort helped me unwind and took my mind off things.

At long last the sun sunk behind the hill and I gratefully welcomed the arrival of the evening.

I had taken my shoes off in readiness for the wish-fulfilling ritual, just as Maria instructed me to do. That way, I would be in direct contact with the earth and the nature around. Contrary to modern sensibility, that way of thinking was no stranger to me: Grandma Gafia taught me once that working in nature is a way of life which connects you with the whole Universe. In fact, I would usually see her taking her shoes off before stepping into her garden to cut the grass and work the land. To her, work was worship, and nature was her church. That's how much she respected the land.

Following in her footsteps, I did the same, while breathing deeply in and out to calm my nerves. I was sure that Maria would make an appearance any moment to take her turn and have her dreams come true. Knowing her, she wouldn't have missed the chance for the world!

After a wait which felt long and draining, I started fretting about wondering why Maria wouldn't show up. The dark became more intense with every second that passed, and a cold sweat covered my entire body; I was out at night, on my own, not far from Auntie Vera's cottage and all the terrible stories Maria had ever told me began to come to life.

I stared around and caught sight of the dried-out beanstalks in Auntie Vera's fence. I trembled with anticipation as I expected the fence to suddenly turn into the life-threatening thorny barrier that would separate Auntie Vera's cottage from the world around. In a moment of panic, I looked up at the sky for a morsel of courage, and I saw the Evening Star shining down on me like a beacon of hope. It might have been the funny way that I blinked or something of the kind, because I genuinely thought that the Star beckoned at me from above. When I peered around again, the thick lilac bush growing near the wall of the house was draped in a silvery moonlight. The grasshoppers were getting warmed up for their nocturnal concert and up in the night sky, the moon had just come out from behind a fluffy cloud. I took it all as a good sign.

I plucked up the courage and sped up towards the pear tree. Great hopes were hanging on the outcome of my adventure! My heart was pelting in my chest and my bare feet hesitated for a moment as I stepped in something soft lying on the ground. My eyes, however, never left the sight of the magic tree, so I instinctively knew I was not yet within reaching distance of it. I edged forward until I could touch the warm trunk as I put my arm out, allowing myself to sense its vibration like a telepathic acceptance of what was still to come. Once the close contact established, I started slowly walking around the pear tree, uttering a wish with every full spin.

"Please, St George, make Nadia well again," I said for my first wish.

The shadow of a bird flying across the sky in the night distracted me for a moment, but the memory of the white eagle in my dream abated my brief unrest. I carried on summoning St George to fulfil my wishes. In the meantime, I couldn't help noticing the warm, soggy texture of the soil around the pear tree. Totally engrossed in cajoling the stuff dreams are made of into becoming reality, I chose to also believe that everything around was transformed by the magical touch of the moment. Moreover, to keep away the worldly distractions, I decided to close my eyes and block out any little detail which would come between me and the realization of my dreams! By that stage, my legs would sink up to my knees into the soft boggy ground around the tree and the strong ripe smell rising from it couldn't be ignored for much longer!

Determined to stick to my oblivion to the world in favor of my focus on the magic of the moment, I counted in my mind the number of spins around the tree that came with as many granted wishes. All along, I kept chanting in a loud voice:

"Please, St George, let such and such be done…"

Just as I was going around the third time, my stomach started turning and my head went dizzy and foggy. The stench was overpowering. Yet, I had seven more spins around the tree…

I opened my eyes with a heavy heart for I suspected any undue interruption would have impinged on the success of the wish-fulfilling ritual. Although my good senses forewarned me, I soon had to admit that my naivety had gotten the best of me! Maria, that devil of a girl, was, of course, at the heart of it all!

I had the instant realization of what had happened and an unstoppable urge to get myself out of there as quickly as possible. I couldn't get clean quickly enough!

Later on, I was to find out that my father had serviced the outdoor toilet, spreading the human waste at the roots of the fruit trees in the garden. Springtime being an early time in the year, allowed for all these 'dirty jobs' to be done with a certain discretion as the garden was not very much transited or used. Besides, it provided the trees and other crops with the natural food they needed.

The day before I had joined Mom working in the field, which gave Dad the space and opportunity to get the job done. The only one who had stayed at home to look after the house was Maria. Apparently, that allowed her with enough spare time on her hands to cook up her next prank for me!

Everything worked out for her down to the tiniest detail: my legs were soiled up to my knees and it felt as if the dirt and stink were soaked into my skin for good. I could have cried out loud with desperation and disgust! It was all too much for me!

A jingly laughter traveled from the porch to the garden, scaring away a few birds in a tree and covering the sound of the grasshoppers for a few seconds. Maria had seen the whole thing and was now killing herself laughing. Her plan had paid off handsomely and she had me fooled by the book!

I stooped down to grope for some soft earth balls which I could throw at her. By the time I stood up again, she had already taken off! I could have killed her then and there if she dared come near me! And she knew that! As she was running away, I heard her saying:

"You swore on your beauty spot that you'll tell no one about it!"

That was hardly a good time for her to be smart with me: in my blind fury I had forgotten everything about my vow and my beauty spot! If I could, I would have gotten rid of my own legs, that's how repulsed I was! Seeing me in such a state, Maria understood it wasn't a good time for reasoning and bargaining, so she jumped the fence back into the garden and dashed for the house, locking the door behind her! It was going to be a while until my anger subsided. If she knew me at all, Maria had worked that one out pretty quickly; the safest way for her to be was out of my way!

I was trying to think on my feet and get myself cleaned as soon as possible. I rubbed my legs with soil and fresh grass and then I headed straight to the water tap at the back of the garden to give myself a good wash. But Maria had thought of everything: the tap was so tightly turned off that I could not use the water. The stench had become unbearable; I didn't care about anything anymore: my fear of Auntie Vera and her evil witchcraft had disappeared, and so had my fear of the dark! I zipped off to a certain spot in the fence where a loose plank would easily slide off and let me get out and I didn't stop running until I reached the canal.

As soon as I felt the cool kiss of the water touching my legs, my anger started to melt away. The calming embrace of the water rippling around my knees brought peace to my mind and gave me the chance to think about what I stood to lose if I gave in to my temper: after all, I had sworn on my beauty spot not to tell anyone! I also knew deep down inside that I was as guilty of it as Maria: in my naivety, I had chosen to believe everything she told me without questioning! It wasn't an easy pill to swallow, but you live and learn! Last, but not the least, I would have looked like a right pickle in front of the others if they found out! Adding insult to injury was not something I fancied for myself, especially after all I had been through!

Many years later, at one of our family gatherings, I told everybody about it and we all had a good laugh! Through a strange coincidence, that occasion was also a St George's Day celebration!

The Joys of Childhood

Why did Maria insist on getting me to swear on my beauty spot and why was I so reluctant to do it in the first place? Those questions open up a new chapter set to reveal a few things dear to my heart.

My fascination with my own beauty spot stems from a very early time in my childhood. Almost from as early as I can remember, I regarded this feature as my birthright; I'd spend hours in front of the mirror looking at my spot from all possible angles. In time, it had become my signature feature which guaranteed my status as a unique human being in the world. The idea had been planted in my mind by a legend which Mom once told us.

As a result, I had developed a certain pride. I guess I secretly saw myself as being head and shoulders over my siblings, having it confirmed and labeled by the special mark on my right cheek. My infatuation with my beauty spot did not go unnoticed with my brothers and sisters, especially with Maria. The first thing I would do every morning was to go and look in the mirror, making sure that it was still there: I wouldn't have wanted it lost in the bedding or, even worse, left behind in a dream which I had dreamt overnight! And there were plenty of dreams where I battled terrible monsters while carrying on through storms and blizzards and horrible gales! Luckily, my beauty spot would always be there. Pleased to find it in its place, I would gently stroke it and talk to it about my worries and fears. Like all lucky charms, my beauty spot would return the favor not only by enhancing the Charming-Prince glow (which I was born with, anyway!), but also by turning my night terrors into happy thoughts. Speaking of which, I was going to find out later on in life that it was a special gift which only the Evening Star could bestow upon a few chosen ones.

How did it come to this, however? Perhaps my mom's gift for telling stories had something to do with it. I can recall like it was yesterday, one evening around the fire when she told us a story to do with a special mark on the cheek, very much like mine.

My mom was great at spinning a good yarn and she would often get her inspiration from real life and from the people around her. Although she never had time to sit down and read, she seemed to be able to suck up the fun and the oddity of everyday events and throw them into a story at a drop of a hat. Thus, all of us, her children, would take turns in playing the main character in her stories.

She didn't always have time to tell us stories, but on the very special occasions when she would sit down with us to do so, we would make sure that we kept her there for as long as we could.

On that particular evening, which I am going to tell you about, the magic was in the air: the sky was high and starry as if lit up by millions of bright lights. Perhaps our excitement was catchy, and the stars shone with curiosity for the new story Mom had for us!

The Legend of the Beauty Spot

Being a seasoned parent by then, Mom knew that the mischief of children could be a great source of learning new things and mistakes were easier corrected by story-telling than they would be by off-telling.

Mom started her story by introducing to us a large family of ducks. Unlike us who were two brothers and four sisters, the ducklings in the story were five sisters and their busy baby brother, Rica. When she said the name of the baby duckling, Mom looked at me and tapped the tip of my nose with her finger, as if to endear her character to me. I nodded my head in approval, eager to hear the rest.

"… and Rica, the duckling baby brother, although very much loved by her sisters, was never taken seriously by them," Mom explained.

"But why won't they take him seriously?" I asked promptly.

"You'll soon find out if you listen carefully…"

"Have you told this story to my sisters before?" I whispered trying not to be heard by the others.

"What do you think?" Mom toyed with me. I shrugged my shoulders. I felt a bit nervous which put a knot in my throat.

"Of course, I haven't told them this story before…" Mom smiled and kissed me on the crown of my head.

That really made my day and put a smile on my face. I felt my ears burning with excitement, like two small red roses dotted with dewdrops. I looked up at the sky, but not a raindrop in sight! It was just me sweating with anticipation!

My sisters exchanged glances amongst themselves. They could tell from a mile that Mom and I would be accomplices in the making of the story. They could enjoy everything as the audience, but the stage was just for the two of us that night! Cheeks flushed, sparkle in my eyes and an inability to sit still gave it all away for me! I liked ducks, I found them funny, and I loved ducklings, especially this one who was the youngest in his family, just like me! It didn't take much for me to identify with the little duckling. This story was all about me, I had decided! I knew Mom's story was going to be a hit!

Mom smiled. In moments like this, her calling as a mother shone through. What could be more rewarding than a cheeky face frozen still in expectation for a miracle to happen. And a miracle her stories were!

"So... where was I?" Mom challenged me.

"Once upon a time there was a family of ducks and the baby duck was called Rica! Just like our family!" I burst out in a breath.

"That's right..." she agreed in a soft voice which soothed me.

The flame of the candle swayed from side to side and the acacia tree in the front of the window cast its long shadow inside, ready to listen to the story. That tree had been there for as long as I could remember, and we regarded it as the loyal guardian of our household, the one who took upon itself the thick of the bad weather, both in scorching temperatures and in freezing cold! Our acacia tree had always been our loyal protector against the whims of nature.

That evening, however, even the acacia tree stood there mesmerized, swaying its strong branches this way and that way in the gentle breeze. For a moment, I imagined those big gnarly branches moving with the wind as snakes dancing on a tune of a magic flute. Trying to make their way in through a window cracked open, the slithering snakes seemed to settle down once Mom's voice raised gently over the rattle of the wind stirring outside...

"Are you still listening?" Mom checked on me.

"I'm all ears, Mom." I assured her, finally taking my eyes off the strange shadows which filled the room as if battling amongst themselves for a better place in the audience, ready to listen to Mom's story. "Why wasn't Rica taken seriously by his older sisters? Even though he was younger than them, he was still their brother..." I elaborated my question.

Mom smiled quietly content. Her story had already started to work its way through our minds, raising questions, suggesting answers, leaving behind valuable teachings. Mom never pointed fingers and made it explicit in her storytelling who should learn lessons and unlearn bad habits; she would recount everything as if she'd heard it from someone else the day before. But somehow, we, the children, instinctively knew who the main characters were in her stories.

"Well, well... Let's see... Perhaps one reason for that kind of behavior was getting too carried away with oneself... Unfortunately, that usually happens when ignorance and selfishness pair up and become the driving engine in life..." Mom paused for a moment, furtively peeking at my sisters.

Yet, my sisters didn't bat an eyelid over Mom's remark as if that was nothing to do with them. I, on the other hand, was not old enough to grasp the hidden meanings of Mom's words:

"How can selfishness and ignorance become a driving-engine?" I asked puzzled. "Oh, oh, I think I get it now: you mean to say that people can get really big-headed, they think they know it all and start doing naughty things!" I finally made sense of Mom's words.

"That's exactly what I mean to say!" Mom agreed tapping again the tip of my nose with her finger. There must have been the trace of a questioning stare which made her carry on:

"Children, do you know when mirrors came in use?" she moved her look from me to my sisters who glanced at each other surprised, not knowing what to say and not quite able to understand what the connection to our story was.

"No idea…" they admitted half-heartedly.

By coincidence, one of my sisters was holding a little mirror in her hand just in case she needed to check on the state of her hairdo at any time.

"You should know that mirrors have come in use when people started feeling lonely for the first time."

The girls peered at one another quickly.

Mom peeked at the icon on the wall lit up by the flicker of the candle burning underneath it, a pair made in heaven.

"Nobody needed mirrors beforehand, because people used to look in each other's eyes and see their souls in all their beauty. In fact, the joy of seeing someone as they truly are, is a rare commodity nowadays, and the illusions of mirrors have always proved nothing but disillusion!"

Mom's eyes rested on me and, seizing the opportunity, I tried to catch sight of my own reflection in them. But the light of the candle was too weak, and I couldn't see anything besides the projection of the shadows which lingered on Mom's face like a crowd of uninvited guests crashing a private party. Mom sighed and shuffled on the spot, which made the shadows withdraw in a hurry and let the candle light shed a glint on her face. Her eyes reflected back the flame and I took the opportunity of looking straight at her; Mom's eyes mirrored a glowing microscopic image of myself which held the full meaning of her words.

"Can you say that again?" I asked her to repeat.

"The eyes are the mirrors of the soul, my dear boy," she explained. "You can see in them the whole beauty, or the reverse of it, as it is the case with each of us! With the coming of mirrors into the world, we are under the illusion that a piece of glass can show us the beauty we long for. But we forget that in order to become a mirror, a piece of glass goes through changes and suffering, and when the mirror is ready to hang on the wall, we'll have to be ready to pay the price for our vanity…" Mom peeked at my sisters and released a slight sigh.

"How do we pay the price for our vanity?" my sisters ventured the question whisperingly.

"We pay the price for our vanity by buying into the illusion which the mirror reflects back at us… It's a subtle, but effective revenge… An illusion that creates confusion; we get so carried away with whatever we see in the mirror, that we soon get to believe it is the reality!”

“How can you say that a mirror distorts our image, Mom?” Maria challenged her as usual.

“My dear girl,” Mom replied in a soft voice, “a mirror is an inanimate object, while you are a distinct human being with feelings and thoughts… You must be very naïve to put your trust in a piece of glass.”

“But why wouldn’t I trust it! I look in my mirror and I like what I see…” Maria rebelled.

“My dearest, you’ve just said it yourself: *you* like it! This is nothing to do with the mirror!”

“Isn’t it?” my other sisters appeared surprised.

“Not at all!” Mom explained. “The image in the mirror is a figment of your imagination first and foremost! It’s nothing but an illusion which, taken the wrong way, can lead you astray and drive you away from everybody you hold dear: parents, siblings, friends…”

“I still don’t understand, Mom!” I complained.

“Love of thyself is the main reason why people give up on one another,” she tried to make me understand.

“Love of thyself?” I repeated not quite sure what to make of it.

“That’s exactly it!” she confirmed.

“Is this all happening because of the mirror?” my sister, who was holding the pocket mirror in her hand, asked shyly while discreetly placing it down. Then she scrutinized our faces for a reaction.

“It’s not all down to the mirror!” Mom tried to reassure her with a smile.

“If it’s not the mirror, what is it?” my sister insisted.

“It’s also down to those people who should be there for you to guide and advise you…” Mom explained.

“What’s that to do with them?” my sister looked confused.

“The people who are meant to guide you should warn you about the misleading ways of becoming infatuated with yourself, since the perilous path of arrogance and self-adoration will only put more distance between you and the true meaning of life. In the end, you risk losing your way, you most likely become deaf and blind to your calling in life and miss out on growing as a person and getting to be the best you can be. It’s very much like driving a powerful car but ignoring all the traffic rules which help you stay safe. When you look in the mirror thinking of yourself as the most beautiful girl in the world, the mirror reflects back at you what you want to see…”

“How can love make you do all those bad things? Is there bad love and good love?” I questioned, even more confused.

"My dear boy, love is not good or bad, big or small, sweet or sorrow… Love has no shape, size, taste to it, but it's what people make of it… It's like everything else in life: thoughts are not good or bad in themselves, it's the way we apply them to reality, which makes that difference. When love is selfishly understood and acted upon, people get so engrossed in themselves that they forget about the world around them; they have no time for kindness, for genuine friendship and for caring for their peers. Sadly, this sort of behavior damages everybody, including those who are guilty of it! To come back to our story now, Rica's four sisters were always too busy grooming their feathers and beautifying themselves and had no time for their little brother. Rica tried for a while to do the same in the hope he would stand out to his sisters and they would make more time for him, but it was to no avail."

"Why not?" I asked, eager to find out the answer that would have put me back on track with my sisters who were doing the same as the duck sisters in the story.

"The little ducks were only interested in themselves and nobody else!" Mom made it clear. "For all they cared, Rica could have been invisible!"

"How could he have been invisible? Was he magic!" I fell back in confusion.

"They couldn't be bothered about their little brother!" Mom put it bluntly.

The further on Mom went with her story, the more I could recognize familiar similarities with my situation. Being still young and naïve, however, it didn't cross my mind that Mom was actually borrowing facts from reality, draping them in the attractive cladding of story-telling. One thing was for certain: from that night on, ducks have always been amongst my favorite.

"What did Rica do?" I wanted to know the answer straight away for my own benefit.

"Rica gave up on trying to win his sisters over, and from then on he made sadness his loyal friend."

"Can sadness be a loyal friend?" I said, puzzled.

"It can well be," Mom assured me as she quickly peeked at my sisters who still didn't get the hint.

"I guess you're right…" I muttered under my breath.

"The story goes like this: one day the parents went off to get some food for their six ducklings…" Mom went on with her tale.

"Just like our ducks go to the village canal every day," I chipped in.

"Right you are, Gheorghita!" Mom praised me.

"On that day, Rica felt lonelier than ever as his sisters went about their usual business beautifying themselves in the mirror and being oblivious to the world around. Fed up with being ignored and forgotten about all the time, Rica decided to resort to a desperate measure: he walked to the gate, opened it despite his better

judgment and the parents' advice, and shouted as loud as he could so all his sisters heard him:

"Girls, I've decided to leave home! You never bother spending time with me, anyway, so I suppose it will make no difference whatsoever whether I'm here or not!"

"He reckoned his words would make an impression on his sisters and they would start taking notice of him," Mom commented.

"Did it work?" I enquired shortly.

"He may as well not have bothered!" replied Mom to my disappointment.

The older sisters carried on regardless with their grooming, stepping on each other's toes to get a better spot in front of a mirror, while paying themselves outrageous compliments. The younger ones who had been pushed at the back of the queue, tried to make up for it by peeking at their reflections in the morning dewdrops hanging at the end of the grass leaves.

Rica repeated his words hoping to be heard and taken seriously. He became so worked up that he even stumbled over his own feet and fell over raising a little cloud of dust from the floor and a few hiccups of pain out of his chest. As for his sisters' interest, that stayed solely focused on themselves and nobody else.

Rica stared around him helplessly. A few busy bees started the day taking a bath in a pool of fresh morning dew gathered in a flower cup. Once cleansed and refreshed, they withdrew shyly on a leaf nearby behind a dew-dotted spider-web where they could dry off away from prying eyes. But unlike Rica's sisters, the little bees were very aware of the baby duckling's distress. In fact, one of them stood up and got out of the dew pool, determined to intervene. Luckily, one of his brethren pointed out at the day's work ahead of them and how little time they had left to finish their morning ritual cleansing. Their rules were strict and their schedule tight!

In the meantime, Rica picked himself up, angry and disappointed at his sisters' ignorance. He went out of the courtyard and stood in the middle of the road not knowing which way to go: left, right or straight ahead? Seeing the little duckling so distraught, another little bee put an abrupt end to his morning bath, quickly wrapped a soft leaf around himself as a towel and hyped himself up to bring some justice into the world. But his enthusiasm was short-lived as an older and wiser bee caught his arm just as he was about to take off:

"Don't delay the fulfilling of another's destiny!" he warned his friend.

"I can't bear to see the little one in distress, while his big sisters can't care less..." he explained.

"Don't worry about it! The little one is not on his own, he acts under divine protection even though he appears lost and lonely. A greater destiny waits ahead of him! The less attention he gets now, the more freedom of action he's got on the way of fulfilling his destiny."

"Do you really think so?" his friend asked surprised at the new way of assessing the situation.

"I know so!"

Totally reassured by his friend's appraisal of things, the bee abandoned his towel and resumed his morning bath, his good-disposition reinstated as soon as he found himself immersed in the lukewarm pool of dew.

Rica was still in the middle of the road, thinking what the best move would be next. He felt like going back to the safety of his parental nest, but his pride got the best of him: he couldn't stand the thought of such an embarrassing defeat! He would have appeared a right fool in front of the crowd of little insects getting ready to accompany his sisters to the canal. He breathed in and out slowly to calm his nerves and then suddenly started walking down the road following his own shadow.

He held himself straightfaced for a while, but after a few hundred meters his tears burst out of his eyes, washing away all the angst, upset and anger. Falling on the footpath, his tears were a heartfelt testimony of his longing for love and friendship and the ground received them with gratitude and humility.

Rica started talking to his shadow which had faithfully been there for him since his birth, had never left his side since and was guiding him on his way to who knows where on that day. Rica was mumbling to himself, wiping his eyes and nose at the same time, blissfully unaware of the direction of his walkabout. Despite his heavy heart, teary eyes and dripping nose, he could smell a heavenly fragrance tickling his nostrils. He stopped for a moment and took a good look around for a hint. He couldn't see anything special, but he noticed that his own shadow had an extra pair of wings!

Making an effort, he managed to grope his back but there was nothing there. He opened up his own wings and folded them back, then moved from side to side but the unaccounted-for wings were moving with him! He stood still for a few moments only to discover that the little pair of wings moved on his head, casting his shadow in the shape of an over-sized mouse with big ears and incredibly long, thin tail! Rica lifted his eyes, finally understanding what was going on: a little butterfly was frolicking around him, playing with his shadow and trying to put a smile on the sad duckling's face. It all started when the Butterfly saw Rica marching on the road, talking to himself, but as he joined him in his walk away from home, the Butterfly soon *understood the gravity of the situation and the sorrow which overwhelmed Rica. A sworn enemy to sadness and sorrow, the Butterfly made it his mission on the day to cheer up Rica and to bring smile and laughter back in his life! Thus, he fluttered around turning his shadow into that of an angel first, then making it look like a strange wobbly mouse! The Butterfly would not leave Rica's side for as long as he was in the grip of sadness, for that was the greatest challenge a butterfly could encounter, and our little Butterfly was determined to contend with it."*

"Why are butterflies and sadness at war?" I couldn't help asking Mom.

"Butterflies can't stand sadness because sadness often preys on lonely and impoverished souls and it often comes in disguise as a frail butterfly dressed up in pastel colors.

But Rica was in luck on that day because his new friend, the little Butterfly, was not only pretty as a picture, but also bright as a button. As soon as he caught sight of Rica in his sorry state, the Butterfly understood that the quickest way back to joy was through play and laughter. In no time at all, he got himself on the back on a rebel strand of draught and surged up in the air, circling and looping around the duckling.

The Butterfly harnessed in the gust of wind towards a nearby bush of lavender, picking up the soothing scent on his wings as he shuffled through the blossom. Rica realized that it was the pleasant smell which drew his attention in the first place, and the shadow of a smile fluttered on his face.

Encouraged by a promising start, the Butterfly danced mid-air in front of the duckling, waving hello. But Rica hadn't gotten over his upset yet. He ignored the friendly gesture of the Butterfly, vacantly glancing in space instead.

"Hello, handsome! What's with the long face? Who upset you?" Butterfly started talking to him while still striving to tame the gust of air which kept him gliding up and down. Being a seasoned rider, Butterfly made use of his antennae to guide Wind with and submit its whims to his will. Suddenly, Wind swooped and whooshed and playfully turned up its tail.

"Hey, steady on, fiery!" Butterfly told him off jokingly. "First, let's see what's wrong with this young fellow! Come on, good looking, you can tell me everything about it! Who upset you?"

Just then, a sunray filtered through and lingered on as if waiting for the duckling's answer.

"You can't take sadness as your only fellow traveler on a nice day like this!" Butterfly tried to cajole him into confession.

Rica looked around somewhat surprised as if he really expected sadness to be there in the flesh. How else could Butterfly have guessed his state of mind? Apart from his own footprints and some tiny teardrops trailing back for as far as he could see, there was nothing and nobody that would have given him away. His heart was wildly beating in his chest; he had never ventured so far out of his own home until now. The sun was already in the middle of the sky and a bunch of mischievous rays were letting themselves fall straight on Rica's head, making him hot and bothered. Hardly in the mood to be teased, Rica pulled himself in the shade of a thick bush. Too many new and strange things were happening at the same time, and he didn't particularly enjoy any of them. He felt rather put off, perhaps borderline anxious.

"It's none of your business!" Rica answered in a huff, not quite sure whether Butterfly was taking the mickey at him, or he was genuinely interested in him.

The frustration stirred up by Rica's sisters was taking a toll on others. Rica wasn't himself and his angry tone didn't go unnoticed with Butterfly. Wind, carrying Butterfly, curled itself up and down disapprovingly. Determined to teach the duckling a lesson of good manners, Wind twirled itself into a mini whirlwind. Closing up from behind, the twister almost caught Rica in its midst, when Butterfly jumped in and stirred it away like a true master of the elements, while whispering:

"Gently does it! No amount of twisting and twirling will turn this little duck back to his high spirits! I know just the thing for it!"

With Butterfly in control, Wind lowered its blowing and diffused most of its power to a gentle breeze which woke up the scent of the blossom around. Gathering the best of the scent on its wings, the gust of wind took it and spread it all around the duckling to comfort and cheer him up. But Rica was not easily pleased that day; he reluctantly frowned at the kindness of Wind.

Butterfly, however, had had enough of Rica's bad attitude:

"Listen up, little duck; both Wind and I have been trying hard to cheer you up and all we had from you in return was moody behavior and stubborn rejection. Nothing can be that bad! Don't you think you are taking this a bit too far now?"

Rica was in no reasoning mood, though. He shuffled his tail from side to side, flicked his quiff backwards and walked past Butterfly pretending not to hear a word. Draught curled upon itself, sniffing the scent it carried on the tip of its tail:

"Has the duckling gone nose-blind because of his sorrow, or perhaps he's been senseless all along! That would explain his behavior from head to tail!" Wind commented.

The scent of the Rafiqui flowers and lavender mixed together was a match made in heaven. How could the duckling resist it?

Butterfly winked at Wind and they both flew off chasing after Rica. When they caught up with him, they checked him out and silently agreed that the duckling was, indeed, in a state of acute sadness, a very serious and worrying state. Butterfly guided Wind which soared high up in the sky. With a bird's eye view on the place, he had a good look around trying to work out which one was Rica's house.

Luckily, Rica had forgotten to close the gate behind him, which gave Butterfly the exact location of his house. With that mystery solved, Butterfly put together a plan of action and before he set out on it, he descended briefly to make sure that the duckling was safe and out of danger for the time being.

Finding out what caused the duckling to be so upset was a matter of urgency.

The first sight which welcomed Butterfly was the swarm of bees taking their morning bath in the pool of dew. Needless to say, that both parties looked away in embarrassment; the bees either jumped back in the water, or rushed to grab their towels and cover themselves, while Butterfly steered away and ducked down behind the flower petals to give them some privacy:

"Sorry to disturb you, guys!" Butterfly apologized.

Before long, Butterfly discovered the vain ducklings who were fully engaged in a catwalk show, paying compliments to each other and showing off in front of a multitude of insects which just had their breakfast and were now resting nearby. Butterfly and Wind looked each other in the eye with the instant understanding of what had caused the sorrow of the baby duckling.

"Hello, girls, have you, by any chance, got a little brother?" Butterfly cut to the chase without any other introduction as his eyes rested on the gate which was hanging open blown by a vagrant gust of wind, bustling to and fro with a moaning sound.

But it was all for nothing. Butterfly wasn't even noticed by the ducklings who were busying themselves around praising their own good looks and admiring themselves in the mirror… Wind could feel a storm building up inside him, that's how outraged he was! In a fit of anger, he rushed straight through the middle of the ducklings ruffling their quiffs, turning their aprons back to front and generally creating a hullaballoo…

But it seemed that nothing could distract the ducklings from their impromptu beauty contest. In fact, Wind managed to bring about the opposite effect: excited about their sudden change in appearance, the ducklings rushed over to the nearest mirror to welcome the fashionable twist in the way they looked. They even turned around and said thank you for it! Wind just couldn't believe it! If he wasn't so mad, he would have roared with laughter! He frantically stormed this way and that way.

"What are you looking for?" Butterfly wanted to know.

"I should expect to find a poppy somewhere around here!" Wind explained.

"What do you need a poppy for?"

"I'm beginning to think these ducklings must be on poppy juice. There is no other explanation for the way they are acting! What a bunch of... of..." Wind was hard-pressed to keep it neutral, "... of numpties!" he grumbled.

Butterfly was not yet ready to pack in and give up. He flew over to the eldest duckling to make another attempt. The eldest should have been the most mature, as well. The eldest sister wore a dress which would have been rather pretty if it wasn't so tight on her waist that it hardly allowed her to breathe. She thought it was her duty as a big sister to lead the way when it came to fashion and beauty!

Butterfly landed squarely on her beak to make sure he wouldn't be ignored this time around. Surprised and slightly taken aback, the duckling instinctively crossed her eyes to have a good look at the new arrival. After a few moments of *contemplation, the duckling suddenly realized that Butterfly made a new and original addition to her overall look and rushed over to a clump of vegetation covered in dewdrops to admire herself. Before Butterfly could make a sound, the duckling had worked it all out: with her living accessory on she was by far the most interesting out of them all!*

"Yoo-hoo! Girls! Take a look! Aren't I pretty with the butterfly on?" she called out at the others.

They all stopped whatever they were doing and looked at their older sister. By now, Butterfly had left her beak to make a successful landing at the back of the duckling's head, resembling a colorful bow.

"Wow! How pretty is that!" the rest of the ducklings said.

Butterfly, however, wasn't there to stay and he took to his wings in no time, much to the desperation of the duckling who started shuffling her plumage.

"Don't leave me so soon, please!" she implored. "Come back!"

Riding on the back of Wind again, Butterfly was almost out of sight with a flutter of his wings. He knew everything he needed to know about the upset of the baby duck and what had caused it in the first place!

Back in the garden, the ducklings wasted no time: the unexpected guest inspired them for the morning, and they all hurried on the lawn to pluck off flower petals and stick them on as bows. Seeing the insensitive massacre of the flowers in the name of beauty, the bees in residence started a vehement protest. All the other tiny insects present in the audience—beetles, flies, flees, and lice—swarmed up creating a right hustle and bustle. You would have been forgiven for thinking that an alien abduction was taking place on the spot!

At a fair distance from there, the Butterfly's smooth gliding was brought to an abrupt halt by Wind which decided to stop briefly in mid-air out of the blue.

"Have you lost your mind!" Butterfly told him off as he spread out his wings to restore his balance. He busied himself tidying up the medals on his chest all in disarray, this helped him regain his cool.

The improvised whip, a fine wand cut out of lavender stalk, had dropped onto the ground below and Wind eventually spotted it resting on a red flower which couldn't quite get her head around it and looked at them in a strop.

Reluctant to leave anyone behind bearing the slightest drop of discontent against him, Wind gallantly picked up the whip from the cup of the flower while languidly blowing her a kiss.

Taken by surprise, the little flower felt her petals whither with a strange longing that pulled the strings of her heart. Love was in the air!

Unaware of the sensitive matters of the heart going on around him, Butterfly pushed his Sherlock-Holmes-style hat on his forehead and scrutinized the surroundings for some clues as to what had made Draught stop so suddenly. But nothing captured his attention, so he asked:

"What have you seen?"

With a distracted expression on his face, Wind stared at a fixed point in space. Butterfly followed his look in search for a clue, but all he could see was a small tuft of grass fresh with dewdrops which were sparkling like diamonds in sunshine... The picturesque view didn't convince Butterfly; Wind wouldn't have dropped out of the sky only for that!

"Hey, Wind, can you tell me what's your problem?" he demanded gently waving the whip.

"Why did we go to check out that particular house?" Wind answered with a question.

"Get out of here... Is that it? Why did we go to check out that particular house? Well, let's see..."

"We wanted to know if the baby duck in distress belonged to that family!" Wind answered his own question.

"Right you are!" Butterfly approved of it. "What exactly is your point?"

"My point?" Wind frowned.

"Yes, what are you trying to prove by it?"

"Oh yes, about that..." Wind finally grasped what Butterfly meant, "... well, after having checked out the ducklings in that household, I think we can both agree that they all very much like one another, the baby duck and the girls... But that doesn't mean they are related, does it? What if the baby duck is not their little brother? That would explain why the ducks didn't pay much attention to us!" Wind concluded.

"They are not related? You are joking, right!" Butterfly couldn't believe his ears.

"I'm actually being very serious about it: you couldn't tell one duck from another, just like you couldn't tell a butterfly from another!" Wind argued his point.

Butterfly's doubts had been blown away by Wind's self-assured attitude. He looked behind in the direction of the household they had just visited. A quick glance between them confirmed the thought which crossed both their minds at the same time: they had to go back and settle the matter once and for all!

They turned around and approached the household from one side, taking all necessary precautions to avoid the bees in the air and the ducklings on the ground. Unfortunately for them, a whole swarm of lay-about insects hanging around for the catwalk show spotted them and alerted everybody:

"Hey, everybody, look who's come back! It's the little butterfly from earlier on!"

The ducklings jumped with excitement, the eldest being beyond herself with exhilaration.

"You better give them a good run for their money," Wind suggested with a wink. "Sit yourself here on this Imperial Lily where you can be safely out of reach, but still in plain sight…"

The Imperial Lily was the perfect backdrop for Butterfly. The strong and inviting fragrance which filled the air around was to die for!

"Where are you going?" Butterfly wanted to know.

"I'll go have a look inside, fish around for some clues…" Wind filled him in as he took off.

"Sounds good to me!" Butterfly agreed with a smile.

Wind swooped away and headed straight for the open window to the house. The first thing which stood out to him once inside, was the oversized mirror in the shape of a heart which appeared even bigger against the deep blue of the wall!

Unable to resist the vanity of youth, Wind started twirling and swirling in front of the mirror and noticed a bit of pollen left by the whip of Butterfly earlier. He picked it up on his fingers and spread it all over his body before admiring himself a bit more. He was a most handsome gust of wind without a doubt! As he looked at himself from all angles, Wind caught sight of something else in the corner of his eye. He turned around to see a framed family photograph hanging on the opposite wall. With a satisfied smirk on his face, he danced his way to the wall across the room, his eyes never leaving sight of his beautiful self, reflected in the mirror. When his back eventually touched the wall, he turned around quickly, causing the flame of the candle beneath the icon to go up and down a few times."

"Why was Wind smirking?" I asked Mom.

"All the ducklings in the courtyard were present in the family photograph and Rica, the baby duckling, was resting on his mother's lap happily sucking on a dummy and displaying two very kissable chubby cheeks!" Mom explained with a short laughter. Mom's words pleased me greatly.

"Wind had all the proof he needed.

Rica, on the other hand, had walked off in a huff muttering to himself something about the nosiness of Butterfly:

"Can't he see that I'm not in the mood for anyone? He kept sticking his nose in my business again and again…"

As the duckling waddled further down the road, his attention was drawn by some strange noises. His head automatically pulled backwards to get a better view of the surroundings, but, while doing so, the duckling felt a crackle of grinding bones at the back of his neck. Cautious, he stepped to the side in the shade of an overgrown clump of grass.

He peeped from his shelter and noticed how a newly born flower bud was being nursed by a few young grass leaves. It was hard to imagine how that special little plant got in the middle of nowhere and caught roots in such an unlikely spot. Perhaps it fell from the hungry beak of a bird flying by. With the blessing of new life sprouting out of the seedling, along came the help and assistance which was much needed; the surrounding grass leaves provided the new plant with plenty of dewdrops, sheltered it from the scorching sun and kept it warm from the chill of the night. It was their way of preserving the life of the place and insuring its future: having a rare fragrant plant in its midst meant that entire populations of bees, ladybugs, grasshoppers, butterflies and fireflies would have flocked in and out, carrying the pollen to and fro, and even more importantly, carrying the most beautiful tales to the four corners of the world.

The sudden appearance of the clumsy duckling shattered the harmony of the place. Unaware and trampling over everything, the duckling almost stepped over the young flower bud; luckily, the grass leaves leant over it protectively padding it all around.

Panic-stricken, the duckling skipped a few times before he crashed into a nettle bush, flapped his wings, took off and crash-landed into a bunch of dandelions. The fluffy plants were sun-bathing and, when suddenly presented with the unexpected visitor, they released a few young wispy seeds in the air to celebrate the occasion. Slowly, the fluff glided gently and rested on Rica's bright, yellow plumage, providing the perfect camouflage for him. Grateful for such a warm welcome, Rica shuffled into a most comfortable position and relaxed a bit. A mild breeze floated by, playfully ruffling Rica's feathers and the dandelion fluff altogether. Unsettled by yet another unexpected guest, the dandelion seedlings took off to the wind in celebration formation, trailing like a royal mantle trailing behind the vagrant wind, looking forward to being spread around the width and length of the earth.

The dandelion plants, however, continued to root out for the little duckling, nestling him in their midst whilst giving him the special guest treatment. In his turn, Rica was starting to think that he could get used to being pampered like that more often. No sooner did he get his breath back, when a humongous shadow appeared out of the blue and advanced fast towards the spot where Rica was hiding. At first, Rica blamed it on a low cloud which was trying to get rid of its wet load. Cautious, he peeped in all directions, but saw nothing.

"Could it be Butterfly? He seemed to be a funny guy!" the duckling wondered. "But why would he want to tease me? I've done nothing to him! You wait, smart guy, I'll show you how a duckling can sting like a bee! We'll talk then, from one bug to another!" the duckling tried summoning some courage.

He picked up a few pebbles from the ground in case he needed to defend himself, then stepped slowly out of the dandelion bush and walked to the middle of the road. A few fluffy dandelion seedlings lazily glided off from the mother plant and sat themselves on his head, back and the tip of his tail. Adorned like that, Rica looked the cutest duckling in the world!

Rica scrutinized the horizon for the mischievous Butterfly, but instead a Cuckoo came in sight. It was a fully grown Cuckoo who seemed to search the grounds for something he had lost. He looked a bit put off by the fact that the object of his interest was nowhere to be found, but all of a sudden, his attention was drawn by something worthwhile his attention. From his spot, Rica couldn't see what it was, but he couldn't miss the puzzled expression on the Cuckoo's face. He looked like a guy in the right place at the wrong time...

"Is he looking for me by any chance?" Rica asked himself. "Perhaps my sisters eventually noticed my absence and sent for help..."

Full of hope, Rica stared in the distance in the direction of his house, but there was no commotion to confirm his wishful thinking.

"Or maybe Butterfly alerted Cuckoo about me... Good gracious, I must be going mad!" he scolded himself. "This poor bird must be looking after his own business, *and there is me fantasizing and making up crazy stories..." he puffed and huffed throwing the pebbles away.*

Cuckoo was intently observing Rica but was in no hurry to get chatty.

Rica was not too keen on making contact himself, so he attempted taking off as quickly as possible. On making his way out of there, Rica glanced down at the ground only to notice his own shadow... with some additions. This time it was not a pair of wings, but... He groped the quiff on the top of his head and released the dandelion fluff stuck in there. A quick glance at the mother-plant exonerated him of any guilt with a gentle nod of the head: it was time for the little fluffy seeds to fly the nest and find their own ground to sprout and grow. They were following the order of things set out for them by Mother Nature, a custom as old as the world itself. No wonder these delicate plants spread as far as the eye could see and beyond.

The duckling watched them getting high up in the air on the crest of a little breeze and from there being blown in the distance. He soon lost sight of them but knew in his heart that they would be just fine.

He peered from the corner of his eye at the mother-plant who shook her head playfully and sent a few more seedlings in his direction. With a slight wave of the wing, Rica helped them rise in the air and go with the flow...

When the excitement of seeing new life released into the world subsided, Rica felt somewhat anxious. He decided it was about time he moved on as well. Thus, he tidied up his ruffled feathers and put one foot in front of the other, determined to not let himself side-tracked by anyone and anything.

Hardly had he made the first step on the way to who-knows-where, when Cuckoo planted himself firmly in front of him. Cuckoo was close enough for Rica to see he was carrying a poppy seed in his beak:

"You better step to the side, otherwise I'll tell my daddy about you and he'll put you right..." Rica thought a head-on approach would give him the upper hand. He also ruffled up his quiff to make himself look scary like his dad when he was angry.

"Take it easy, my lad, and don't get uppity with me for no reason..." Cuckoo replied calmly after dropping the poppy seed to his foot.

"Is there anything I can help you with, mister?" Rica wanted to know.

"As a matter of fact, there is, my good lad! But just to put your mind at ease, I'll tell you now that I wish you no harm..." Cuckoo replied.

"Very well then! What is it that you want?" Rica asked bluntly, squinting at the sun to make out that he had no time to waste.

"'Good morning' would be nice for a start!" Cuckoo said diplomatically.

Rica looked up again and commented wisely:

"It's more like midday!"

"Good day to you, in that case!" Cuckoo humored him.

"What if my day is not good at all and I'd rather not talk to you!" Rica pushed it.

"With that attitude, I'm not surprised you've had a bad day so far, and you not talking to me won't best please me, but it will hurt you more than me!"

"Why will it hurt me more than you?" Rica defied him again.

"You will have missed the opportunity to learn something about life, that's why! So, nil points on this occasion!" Cuckoo concluded.

"Nil points for who?" Rica accepted the challenge.

"Nil points for the blissfully unaware!" Cuckoo replied mysteriously.

"For the blissfully unaware?" Rica repeated and stared around to see whether he was talking about somebody else.

But Cuckoo seemed eager to move on since the whole discussion was beyond the point.

"I am actually looking for a little worm about this big…" Cuckoo informed Rica showing him a tiny space between two feathers to size it up for him. "It's not too big, not too small, average size for a worm, well put together, striped tail. Have you seen it?"

"It sounds like a fairly typical worm… Even if I caught sight of it, I wouldn't remember it because I've got other things on my mind…" Rica dismissed the question trying to go around Cuckoo and on his way. "By the way, my parents taught me well to greet my elders, but never to talk to strangers; so, I guess it's game over in favor of the blissfully aware!"

While the duckling and Cuckoo were busy scoring points against each other, a thump could be heard somewhere nearby. Rica's quiff flattened back in fear and he looked ahead, ready to take off from there as quickly as he could.

"I'm not talking about just any worm, my good lad! This one is special…" Cuckoo insisted.

"Special? What do you mean?"

"Very special: it's got a star on its forehead!"

Rica gawped at him in disbelief.

"A worm with a star on its forehead? Why is everybody taking the mickey at me today!" Rica murmured starting to feel sorry for himself.

"Who has been taken the mickey at you today?" Cuckoo suddenly became interested and peeped around for some clues.

"I beg your pardon?" the duckling acted offended.

"Who else have you come across today?" Cuckoo relayed it to him.

"Well, a bit earlier I bumped into…" Rica whispered while sweeping the ground around with a quick glance.

Rica's inquisitive look did not go unnoticed with Cuckoo who became suspicious of the little duckling: his hesitation might have been a sign that he held useful information which he wasn't willing to pass on. As they were both carefully negotiating their way through intelligence-sharing, far behind in the horizon Butterfly showed up still riding on the back of the wind. The colorful Butterfly grew quickly from just a spot in the distance to its normal size, since Wind had chosen to provide the speediest ride ever. Although a seasoned traveler on the wings, Butterfly had obvious difficulty keeping unruly Wind under control. They were flying through the air at full speed like a bullet out of a gun. In fact, they were both worried and concerned for the wellbeing of the duckling they had left behind a while ago.

But as soon as they saw the duckling and Cuckoo engrossed in conversation in the middle of the road, Wind took a sharp turn which threw Butterfly off into a flower cup. A lucky soft landing, indeed!

Left without a rider, Wind took shelter in a bush nearby, well within earshot of the duckling and Cuckoo. It wasn't long before Butterfly realized that somebody else *had found the beautiful flower an attractive location for his morning bath: a ladybug was singing to herself in a low voice while taking a dip in the dew-pool formed at the bottom of the flower cup.*

"Say nothing about our encounter, little duckling!" Butterfly whispered hopefully, ignoring the ladybug who carried on with her morning ritual.

"What are you saying there?" the Ladybug questioned him. "Who's going to say anything about our encounter?" she wanted to know unable to understand what was going on, as she hurried to finish dressing up.

"Shush!" Butterfly implored her.

Ladybug sat next to Butterfly on the same petal and carried on regardless:

"La-la-la! The encounter with a butterfly today. Really, really made my day!"

"Can you keep it down, please!" Butterfly urged her, afraid that the two birds might already have heard him. Acting on impulse, Butterfly covered Ladybug's mouth with a hand while silently pointed towards the road where the two birds continued their conversation. At a discreet peek from behind the petal, they could also notice Wind waving a leaf in their direction from the opposite side of the road. Butterfly cheered up at the sight of his friend.

"So, you were saying about somebody you've met earlier, my good lad…" Cuckoo reminded him

"I only saw a butterfly earlier, but no worms…" Rica informed him.

"A butterfly, you say…" he managed to utter before he choked and coughed violently, while his eyes were fixated on the poppy-seed next to his foot.

A cloud of tiny insects took to the air, scared by Cuckoo's racket, who was all flashed with excitement.

"Yes, that's what I said: a butterfly! What's the big deal?" the duckling couldn't make any sense of Cuckoo's reaction. In his turn, the latter peered around and muttered to himself:

"Could that be? Could he have turned into a butterfly in the meantime?"

"Who are you talking about? Who is he?" Rica was totally confused.

"Which way did he go?" Cuckoo asked another question ignoring Rica's.

The duckling stared at him, baffled.

"I mean the butterfly! Where did the butterfly go, which way?" Cuckoo enquired hastily.

"I think he went… "Rica looked up in the sky, "… or maybe he came from…" and he took a good glance all around. "… to be perfectly honest, I have no idea where he came from and which way he left! All I remember is the butterfly showing in front of me out of the blue. But why are you so interested in a butterfly if you are looking for a worm?" Rica became suspicious.

Cuckoo cast a glance to the left, one to the right and another one towards the duckling.

"Didn't you say it was a caterpillar you were looking for?" the duckling struggled to make head and tail of the situation.

But all the duckling's insistence managed to do was make Cuckoo very uneasy. Irritated to be put on the spot like that by a child, he shuffled from one foot to the other. Rica stepped back cautiously, which warned Cuckoo he was about to lose the morsel of trust he managed to gain so far. He quickly composed himself and addressed the duckling in a reassuring voice:

"Dear boy, can you please humor a poor, old bird and ruffle through your clever young mind for any details about the butterfly? Anything at all! Will that be too much to ask of you? I'd like to find out how he got to have a star on his forehead!"

"Is that all? Nothing else?" Rica exclaimed surprised and somewhat relieved.

"That's all! I swear!"

"You shouldn't envy other creatures for their gifts, nor should you judge them for the way they look or behave, as long as they mind their own business and don't harm anyone," Rica wasn't quite convinced.

"If you must know, I'd like to get a star and give it as a present to one of my children. Fate pulled us apart and I will never be able to be with them. It's the least I can do!" Cuckoo confessed putting on a very sorrowful face.

"Why is that?"

"He was adopted by another family…"

"Adopted!" Rica nearly jumped at the horror of the thought; how could Cuckoo get himself and his son in that situation?

"He was adopted by the family in whose nest I left my eggs…" Cuckoo seemed embarrassed to admit. "It was a special situation, an emergency, really…" he tried explaining.

"An emergency?" Rica echoed the words.

"Yes, I was in mortal danger…"

"Mortal danger…" Rica peeked all around in a state of panic.

"Yes, imagine a whole bunch of vultures hurtling after you…"

Rica's quiff rose in alarm and he felt his knees knocking against each other. In an attempt to stop the trembling, he crossed his legs, which didn't help much, for his tail started shaking visibly. He could still see the clump of kind dandelions in the corner of his eye and calmed down a bit: with a mighty jump he could be back in the safety of their embrace! The mother-plant was gently bobbing its head in the wind, pleased to offer him hospitality again.

"Actually, on second thought, they must have been hawks… So, in the heat of the moment, I managed to safely leave an egg in a strange nest!"

"What did you do with the other eggs?" Rica could hardly breathe.

"Unfortunately, I lost them… I promised to myself then and there that I would be back as soon as I could to recover my egg. But first, I had to get rid of those hawks. I reckon they were on an organized hunt!"

"An organized hunt?"

"Yes! A hunting competition, even!"

"Why do you think that?" the duckling asked.

"It was an awful lot of them in one place. These birds usually hunt alone, vultures and hawks, alike."

Cuckoo droned on and on and sweat drops were sliding along his beak and dropped on the floor.

"Carry on…" Rica encouraged him.

"I managed to stay alive!" Cuckoo trumpeted victoriously.

"That's obvious! What about the egg?"

"What about the egg?"

"It was your egg, carrying your baby!" Rica burst out.

"I made my way back to the nest only to face the mother-to-be…" Cuckoo avoided to make eye contact with Rica and looked in the distance instead.

"And?" Rica urged him to continue while edging forward a bit to catch his every word.

"I didn't have the nerve to go and ask for the egg!"

"Why not?"

"I simply couldn't do it!" Cuckoo lowered his eyes.

"What do you mean? You've given up your egg only because the explanation you had to give her put you out of your comfort zone? Are you… Aren't you… What are you? You are definitely not a good parent!" Rica felt his blood boiling. The shock put Rica at a loss of words.

"Please don't judge me!" Cuckoo pleaded.

"How come you never even bothered arguing your case? You could have explained the situation, anyone would have understood it! This is so wrong on so many levels!" Rica felt he was losing it.

"But, little duckling, before you say anything else, think for a moment: who would give up their child willingly?"

"But that's the whole point: you weren't asking for her child, you were asking for your own child back!" Rica argued.

"That's right, but all eggs look the same! How was I to prove that it was my egg and not one of her own?"

Rica scratched his ruffled quiff; he sensed there was more than met the eye but couldn't quite put his finger on it! Each bird species has its own rules and eggs do seem to look the same, especially when you are a young child. He could tell the situation he was facing mounted far beyond his level of understanding. The first thing which came to his mind was his own family: what if he belonged to another species than his older sisters? That would explain the hard time he had trying to get on well with them.

Rica stood there taking brief suspicious glimpses at Cuckoo who hopped on to get closer to Rica. He had something else to add to his story and didn't want anyone else hearing it:

"You know now why I can't be with my child while he is growing up, but I would like to be able to give them a star as a present on the day when he flies out of the nest for the first time."

"Why wait until he first flies out of the nest and not give him the present on his birthday! All species of birds give their young presents for their birthday!" Rica commented to the desperation of Cuckoo, who was only too eager to get to the end of the discussion but was making a great effort to keep calm and collected until Rica had given him all the information he needed.

"My dear child, the custom of our species has it that on the very first day they fly out of the nest the young should be gifted with a star carried by a certain type of worm and they should also find out the truth about their identity: the revelation of their belonging to the only species of bird who takes its name after its song: the cuckoo! Until then, all our young know about themselves is that they belong to their adoptive family, but it will all be revealed in a moment of blind justice!" Cuckoo blurted out triumphantly.

"A moment of blind justice?" the duckling repeated surprised.

"Yes indeed, my child! The moment must be one when blind justice would prevail, because if justice had any sense of sight, in fact, any sense at all, none of this would come to light! So, you see, my child, discretion is the mother of confession, as the wise say and this particular piece of information must be broken to the young with ultimate discretion!"

"Then perhaps, word on the whereabouts of the butterfly must be accompanied by discretion…" Rica mumbled to himself.

"Very true, my dear boy, I see you are a fast learner!" Cuckoo, who kept a close ear on everything Rica said, picked up on it and tried to ingratiate himself in the hope he would get what he wanted sooner, rather than later.

"Then what?" Rica avoided the sly trap of Cuckoo trying to suck up to him.

"I'll look him in the eye and tell him: you and I are of the same blood and I'm your only family. Listen to the call of our ancestral instinct and dare to fulfil your destiny as a solitary bird, as unique and independent as life itself! But in order for the young to be able to do that, I have to gift him with a little star," Cuckoo explained the importance of the quest he embarked on.

"Oh, that's why the star is so important! I had no idea it holds such powers!" Rica voiced out his thoughts.

"Now you know as much as I do, my child!" Cuckoo continued in a sweet voice almost able to smell the victory at the end of their conversation which he sensed was not far.

Rica looked up and down the road. He had a plan of his own in mind; he turned to face Cuckoo and let him know:

"The butterfly I told you about flew that way!" he said showing the opposite direction than the one he had seen the butterfly leaving for.

In his floral hide-out, Butterfly's jaw dropped in surprise: the duckling kept him safe by setting Cuckoo on the wrong tracks. Butterfly and Wind exchanged glances and smiled at each other; everything was under control! Butterfly's heart hammered in his chest and Ladybug next to him picked up the vibrations in the air. She placed his arm around Butterfly's shoulders in a comforting manner. She would have sheltered Butterfly under her wing, had it not been for the disproportion difference in size, with all the credentials going in favor of Butterfly, of course!

Out there, Cuckoo glared long and hard in the direction pointed out by the duckling. Before he said goodbye, he looked Rica in the eye as if to read his most intimate thoughts, but the duckling didn't bat an eyelid! He knew it was a game of *who-blinks-first but didn't worry a bit: he was a champion in his own right at staring games!*

"Many thanks for your help, child! I'll be on my way after that butterfly now!" Cuckoo eventually said.

Rica's eyes bulged out and Cuckoo added:

"I meant the worm... but I'll check with the butterfly first... Bye for now!" he picked up the poppy seed before spreading his wings and taking off.

Rica shrugged his shoulders, watched him shrinking in the distance, and then cast a goodbye glance at the dandelions on the side of the road. They had enjoyed his visit and he had enjoyed their hospitality, but it was time for the little duckling to go on his way.

A neighboring plant drew the dandelion's attention to Rica's departure and the mother-dandelion plucked up a few fluffy seedlings entrusting them to the tender embrace of the wind to take to Rica as a goodbye gift. A few fragrant petals were also offered as a token of gratitude to the kind gust of wind for the service.

"Very obliged!" the gust of wind thanked them while dashing off to catch up with Rica.

The duckling hadn't made much headway when something from above cast its shadow over him, yet again!

"I hope that cuckoo hasn't come back!" Rica muttered to himself.

Down came a magpie with twin gusts of wind trailing behind her. The three of them looked like right bruisers, the kind you don't want around! In a split second, the twin gusts ambushed the little breeze carrying the dandelion fluff and snatched off the gift meant for Rica.

In his turn, Rica had to stop abruptly since Magpie planted herself firmly in his way. Without any introduction, Magpie started interrogating him:

"What did Cuckoo want from you, little duckling?" she said casting a killer look in the direction where Cuckoo flew.

In the meantime, the dandelion fluff caught up with Rica and cheerfully floated around him.

"You are being spoken to, little duckling, and you better come up with an answer!" she told him off for ignoring her.

Rica eyed her up and down and couldn't help a disdainful thought. If all grown-up birds were like this, his sisters had every excuse to behave the way they did!

"Nothing… Cuckoo didn't want anything from me!" Rica snubbed her.

"Don't even try to give me cheek, do you hear me, boy! I was sitting right there, in that silver beech tree, and I saw you talking for ages. You couldn't have spent all that time talking about… nothing!" she replied offended.

Rica contemplated the size of the bird in front of him and worked it out fairly quickly that he wasn't going to get rid of her unless he gave her what she wanted.

"OK, OK, I don't know… he was looking for someone…" Rica admitted.

"Who was he looking for? Who?" Magpie nearly hopped on top of the duckling with excitement. Rica stepped back, startled.

"Please, dear boy, don't leave me hanging! I'm depending on you!" Magpie implored.

"What are you saying? How are you depending on me?" Rica replied puzzled.

"My wellbeing in my old age depends on your answer!" she informed him out of the blue.

"Your wellbeing in your old age?" Rica had a sinking feeling.

"Please tell me now who Cuckoo was looking for!" Magpie insisted.

"For goodness' sake, he was looking for a worm with a star on its forehead!" he said with a gasp.

"What a scoundrel! What an unbelievable scoundrel!" Magpie burst out in outrage.

Rica pulled backwards in a state of shock at Magpie's outburst of fury. She was now hopping on the spot staring in the distance where Cuckoo had vanished, to the great amusement of a few little plants chuckling on the side of the road. Older and wiser plants, however, nestled in a protective cuddle the dewdrops who started shivering in distress. Rica, on the other hand, stood there petrified and unable to make sense of things.

"I've lost count of the many occasions when I told him to stay out of my business!" Magpie trumpeted her anger as she plucked some feathers and circled around her tail in the middle of the road. She was determined for everybody to find out what a low character Cuckoo had proven to be.

"I've had enough of him! I can only take so much grief from him!" she flapped her wings in discontent.

"If he wants a star, then a star he shall have! I'll make dead sure of it!" Magpie opened up her wings and took off in a huff without even saying thank you to the duckling. Rica shook his head in disbelief and mopped his forehead getting rid of the few droplets of sweat which popped up there, then he carried on his way.

As soon as Magpie lost herself behind the horizon, Butterfly got up, ready to fly off from his hide-out to follow Rica. To his surprise, however, he noticed Ladybug imitating his every move with the clear intention of accompanying him.

"What do you think you are doing, if I may ask?" Butterfly raised his eyebrows questioningly.

"What does it look like I'm doing? I'm coming with you!" Ladybug answered candidly.

"No, really, what are you doing?" Butterfly called out, startling Wind which was getting ready himself to make a dash after the duckling.

"We need to spend some quality time together as you said we would!" she fluttered her eyelashes in his direction. "Now that I've had my bath I feel all fresh and smell like a rose!" she added taking out a perfume dispenser and puffing some on herself. "Want some?" she invited Butterfly who pulled back quickly.

"No, thank you, I'm fine!" he shook his head.

"It's bluebells fragrance! You can at least try some!" Ladybug seemed offended.

"I wouldn't mind trying some, but I'm afraid that might stir up unwanted rivalry!" Butterfly explained politely.

"What kind of rivalry?" Ladybug didn't understand.

"By dint of my nature, I'm supposed to fly from flower to flower irrespective of their size, color, or fragrance; wearing bluebells fragrance will only cause upset and offence to other flowers!"

"When you put it like that, it makes sense!" Ladybug lit up.

Just as Butterfly was launching himself in chatting up Ladybug, a shadow from above cast itself over the flower they were sitting in. It lay itself down over the tiny feet of Butterfly, as if attempting to delay his departure. Suddenly, the flower which offered them sanctuary seemed to become an even more welcoming place. After a quick searching look, Butterfly discovered a busy bee who had sat herself on a petal; she was carrying on her arm a dainty basket, cleverly woven out of the finest spider-web. Whistling cheerfully, she took out of her basket a smart little apron and put it on. The embroidery on it spoke for itself: her husband's portrait was beaming a large smile from the middle of a sunflower, skilfully placed in the middle of a field of roses. It wasn't long before she noticed Butterfly and Ladybug and greeted them:

"Good day to you, love-bugs! Sorry to disturb you, I'll be off now and leave you to it!"

"No, no, you've got it wrong! No need for you to go! In fact, you are more than welcome to stay and do your work and this lovely Ladybug will happily help you out!" quick-thinking Butterfly hatched out a plan to get himself out of a pickle, while casting a languid glance towards the unsuspecting Ladybug. "I can tell you now that you won't find a better person for the job: she is full of life and cheerful, ready to join in whether it's a classic or the latest tune, strong enough to carry your basket and free up your hands for work, the best companion ever! Besides, this arrangement really works both ways as she feels at a bit of a loose end now!" he added winking at Ladybug.

"Fine with me! I couldn't wish for better!" the busy bee agreed instantly.

Before Ladybug could say yay or nay, Butterfly and the bee reached an understanding which made Ladybug a full-time employee for the rest of the honey season.

"This is for the best, my darling!" cheeky Butterfly reassured her. "Never forget this blessed day when happiness came fluttering by and knocked at your door!"

"Happiness fluttered by and knocked at my door?" Ladybug couldn't help but smile bemusedly.

"That's exactly it! I couldn't have said it better myself! And what's more, it all ends happily ever after, with a good and reliable job that will keep you busy and boost up the honey production for this kind bee and, last but not least, release me from any commitment which I might have unwittingly gotten myself into!"

"I'll gladly give you a helping hand, Busy Bee!" Ladybug kindly accepted.

"Great! Never in a million years would I have thought to strike such good luck today! The two of us are sorted out, but what are you going to do?" Busy Bee turned to Butterfly.

"I've got an unfinished job to take care of, but I'll be back as soon as I get it out of the way!" Butterfly promised winking again in the direction of Ladybug.

"I'll be waiting for you right here, handsome! I'll be faithfully watching out for your return through thunders and hail, battling the hardship of nature for your sake!" Ladybug got carried away.

"Got that, Ladybug, through thunders and hail!" Butterfly repeated somewhat scared at the enormity of the promise he had made without much thought (not again!).

"It's a date then!" Ladybug applauded excited at the idea.

"So it is, right here on the spot!" Butterfly called out as he took off.

Busy Bee went back to work straight away while humming a tune to give herself a pace of work and keep the flower she was harvesting happy. She stopped from singing now and again to give little bits of advice and directions to the Ladybug who diligently kept up with her. Bee noticed that from time to time, when she thought nobody would see her, Ladybug sneaked longing glances in the direction where Butterfly had disappeared. To take her mind off things, Bee asked her: "Do you recognize the tune that I've been humming?"

"I beg your pardon? Oh, yes, the tune…" Ladybug came back to reality, "… I know it very well."

"Really? Where did you learn it?" Bee was genuinely surprised.

"I used to live next door to a beehive when I was growing up!"

"That's a fortunate coincidence! Would you like to sing it together?"

"Of course, I would!" Ladybug agreed.

They both started singing in harmony which soon attracted a whole swarm of small insects who, on the spur of the moment, formed a choir and joined in. The sunshine together with the happy songs filled the place with a fairytale atmosphere. Some bugs and beetles even helped gathering pollen and nectar, while others were simply enjoying themselves. The general good mood made everybody feel that time had stopped ticking away and an eternal state of happiness and joy replaced it! For as long as the party carried on, everybody there felt grateful to be part of such a bliss for they knew the memory of it all would stay with them forever and would always guide them like a shining star through darkness…

The sun shone down over the whole nature and, one by one, all the flowers opened their petals to soak in the heat, the songs and the zest for life which were freely floating in the air.

Rica, the wandering duckling who had been part of the scenery for a while, kept walking until he heard a strange noise. He stopped abruptly in his tracks and checked out the ground around. He looked up to see if another mischievous gust of wind was playing tricks on him. Nothing seemed to confirm his suspicions. Rica closed his eyes and breathed in and out a few times to get rid of the overwhelming anguish he felt inside. When his unrest subsided a bit, he opened his eyes again and went closer to the side of the road to examine the delicate blue flowers swaying this way and that way in the wind. The light blue was dotted by pale white marks in some places as if a playful bunch of dandelion fluffs had left their footprints as they were going by. Rica carefully dislodged a few petals and tied them together to make a headdress which would protect him from the sun. He had seen his sisters doing it countless times in the past and was now thankful that, at least, it came to some good! As he braced himself for a long march in the sun, Rica heard the noise from before again. This time, Rica could hear the noise clearly and identified its source: a nearby bush. Stealthily stepping towards it, Rica went in through the side and to his surprise, discovered a red-plumage baby chicken lying down asleep. It was a little cockerel, not much older than himself, who looked like he was taking his midday nap. Having fallen fast asleep in the glaring sun, however, seemed like a very unusual thing to do!

"Strange noises coming from a baby cockerel who seems fast asleep!" Rica muttered to himself staring around in case there was something else. "That's a daring thing to do for a chick, being on his own in the middle of nowhere! Maybe he started off like me; he felt a bit sad and lonely, left his home in search for a friend and stopped here to have a rest…"

Hardly had Rica finished his thought, and the all familiar noise by now could be heard again! Upon closer look, Rica discovered a minuscule worm struggling to get out from under the chick's wing. The effort and the hard work he was putting into his struggle resulted in terrible wind which he was breaking every so often when the pressure couldn't be released in any other way.

On his tiptoes, Rica edged towards the sleeping Cockerel, while making eye contact with the little worm who was silently giving thanks for the unexpected arrival of the duckling. From where he was standing, all Rica could see was Little Worm frantically beckoning at him to keep quiet and not wake up Cockerel. Rica stepped forward and nearly passed out: he could clearly distinguish a star on Little Worm's forehead, just like <u>Cuckoo</u> had mentioned. Could it be…?

"Hey, you, listen up, I've got something to tell you…" Rica said, but stopped when a neighboring bush started shaking and rustling as if somebody hidden there were making themselves comfortable in the place.

At the same time, Cockerel began stirring and Rica gaped at Little Worm in fear for his safety.

"Shush! Please be quiet!" Little Worm implored Rica.

Rica shuffled next to Cockerel and noticed for the first time that Cockerel's comb was bleeding. With slow and gentle motions, Rica lifted Cockerel's wing to help free up Little Worm. The chick moved again, and Rica cautiously lowered Cockerel's wing, mindful of the safety of Little Worm still trapped underneath. Comfortable again in his position, Cockerel relaxed. Rica turned his attention to Little Worm:

"How on earth have you got yourself in there?"

"Shush!" Little Worm implored for silence once more.

Next, Little Worm pulled closer a random leaf lying on the ground nearby and drew on it a flying bird who carried a poppy-flower head in its beak; a little frightened caterpillar was sticking its head out through a tiny hole in the middle of the poppy-flower's head. A microscopic poppy-seed had been thrown at the bird's nostril and an almighty sneeze caused the bird to drop its load on the head of a cockerel passing by down on the ground. That explained the bleeding wound in Cockerel's comb and the uneasy position Little Worm found itself in.

"The flying bird in your drawing, was it a cuckoo by any chance?" Rica wanted his suspicions confirmed.

"It was a cuckoo!" Little Worm agreed whisperingly.

"Was that your home?" Rica asked showing the poppy-flower head in the drawing.

"Yes, indeed..." Little Worm confirmed with a sigh.

"... and the bird passing by underneath was Cockerel here?"

"Yes, yes and yes..." Little Worm agreed sulkily.

Rica had the whole picture now: Cuckoo was after Little Worm who was now struggling to keep his head down in case the confused Cockerel woke up and decided to eat him.

"One thing is for sure: he's not dead..." he voiced out his thoughts.

Thinking on his feet, Rica swiftly lifted Cockerel's wing and this time managed to pull itself from underneath and out he was, heading straight towards a clump of green grass a few feet away.

Perhaps sensing the unusual movement around, Cockerel opened his eyes and saw Rica upholding his wing.

"Hi there!" Rica called out letting go of the wing.

"Hi!" Cockerel half-answered unsure of the situation. He stumbled back on his feet and felt his bleeding comb, letting out an involuntary moan of pain.

"Was it you who attacked me?" he questioned Rica while having a good look around for something he could grab in self-defense.

"Not at all!" Rica denied, hurriedly scared he might have landed himself in trouble again.

"How can you explain this then?!" Cockerel raised his voice and grabbed Rica's breast coat.

Fully coming to, Cockerel peered all around in case others were spying on him. He also felt his pockets to make sure that all his worldly goods were still in place. Rica watched him vexed.

"I have no idea what's happened to you! I really don't! You've got to believe me!" Rica pleaded.

Slipping a furtive look towards the bush where Little Worm was hiding, the duckling could see the little creature silently imploring for his discretion. Rica reassured him with a casual nod.

"Why should I believe you?" Cockerel challenged him. "You seem to be the one and only living creature around as I woke up, which makes you the main suspect as well!" Cockerel concluded.

"Why would that make me the main suspect?" the duckling protested. "What have I ever done to deserve this?" Rica complained trying to free himself from the grip of the Cockerel who was holding on to him for dear life.

"Since you are the only soul in sight, there is no one else to blame it on!" Cockerel confidently exhibited his detective skills.

The quick-thinking duckling groped his secret pocket where he kept a bit of food in reserve to have it for an emergency. His grandparents had taught him well: always keep back a few seeds, especially when you don't know where your next meal is coming from. Rica grabbed the lot out of his pocket and laid them in front of the chick who blushed, pleasantly surprised.

"There you are… These seeds dropped on your head and knocked you out…"

"I beg your pardon?" Cockerel couldn't believe his ears.

He pecked at the seeds, weighed them in his beak for a few moments and then looked Rica in the eye as if demanding an explanation.

"Perhaps a bird flying by dropped them by accident, or…" Rica struggled to find a logical explanation.

"What are you talking about?"

"… or maybe the flying bird saw you wandering aimlessly through the bushes and thought you were a poor orphan looking for food and dropped a few seeds to keep you going…" the duckling mumbled.

At that very moment, Wind picked up the leaf where Little Worm had withdrawn and lifted it to eye-level for the duckling and Cockerel to have a good look at. The poor Little Worm nearly fainted in his bushy hide-out and Rica shifted from one foot to the other, not knowing what to do next. He started whistling while intently staring at a spot behind Cockerel. Distracted by Rica's mannerisms, Cockerel peeked behind him, curious to see what distracted Rica. Seizing the opportunity, the duckling grabbed the leaf and, for a split second, felt at a loss. Luckily for him, Little Worm came to his rescue: he started mimicking feeding himself a leaf. Rica snapped out of his stupor and stuffed the whole leaf in his mouth, almost chocking himself to death on it. When Cockerel moved his attention back to Rica, he was met by two bulging tearful eyes and a croaky voice:

"I can't think of any other logical explanation…"

Feeling a sharp pain, Cockerel shook his comb and a droplet of blood trickled all the way down to his beak.

"So, you are telling me that all those seeds you've just produced out of your pocket fell from the sky and knocked me out?" Cockerel questioned Rica's logic.

"There was a trail of seeds which led me to you and the very last seed in the trail rested on your chest..." the duckling made up an excuse to go along with the previous story.

"Is this how you found me?"

"Yap," the duckling felt compelled to agree. "I was only trying to help you..." he muttered swallowing hard as his throat was still aching from gulping down a whole leaf.

"I thought I struck gold with each seed that led me to the next one, and I couldn't give thanks enough for my good luck." Rica carried on.

"Is that what really happened?" Cockerel was still debating with himself whether he should believe Rica's story; something didn't quite add up, but he couldn't tell what it was.

"Believe it or not, that's what really happened!" Rica emphasized dramatically.

"I don't know what to believe anymore... I only got one wound and there is an awful lot of seeds here... I'm thinking maybe you can't..."

"What? What is it that I can't?" it was Rica's turn to question.

"Maybe you can't count?!"

"Of course, I can count!" Rica was offended. "What kind of silly talk is this?"

Cockerel went quiet, worried for the first time that he might have hurt the duckling's feelings.

"I was a bit surprised to come across such yummy seeds here in the middle of nowhere, to begin with..." the duckling replied a bit embarrassed. "They were too good to leave... so I gathered as many as I could see, but when I was about to continue my journey, a strange noise drew my attention..."

"A strange noise?" Cockerel echoed Rica's words.

At hearing that, Little Worm involuntarily covered his bum with the palms of his hands and hid behind a leaf; he had been the source of the strange noise. In his defense, however, the inert wing of Cockerel lay across his tummy forcing out the gas caused by the stressful situation he was in.

"I followed the strange noise into the bushes and that's how I found you," Rica explained. "You were groaning and moaning, and I couldn't bring myself to continue on my way until I knew you were out of the harm's way and being mistaken for a thief is all the thanks I get for it! I'm just grateful that the fox I saw earlier had gone the opposite direction!"

Worm let out a sigh of relief: his secret was safe!

"Fox! Did you say fox!" Cockerel ducked down instinctively losing grip of the duckling's coat.

"Yes, you've heard me well: I'm talking about the local fox, a sly, ginger madam with some sharp teeth on herself..." Rica emphasized while tidying up his ruffled plumage.

"OK, OK, I got the idea, no need to rub it in! I know what the local fox looks like..." Cockerel replied in a strop.

"You are a fine one to talk, calling me a thief and a robber earlier..." Rica took the opportunity to pay him back.

"Point taken, and if it's any help, I apologize... There you are!" Cockerel held out the seeds for Rica who picked them up and stuffed them back in his pocket.

"We better get out of here soon... The sly, ginger madam might be here any moment... You know what they say: no sooner you say a fox's name, and you become her game!" the superstitious Cockerel said fearfully.

Rica could tell from his high pitch that Cockerel was really annoyed.

"Yes, whatever you say... Let's get out of here," Rica agreed.

Rica turned around, ready to set out with Cockerel. He cast one last look sideways and caught a glimpse of Little Worm discreetly beckoning thank you from the bush where he was hiding, and Rica winked back in response. Cockerel was already ahead of him and the duckling sped up.

Hardly had they taken a few steps, when Butterfly, carried by Wind, suddenly showed up in front of them, frantically fluttering his wings as if chased by a wild beast. Cockerel nearly jumped out of his skin and only the duckling's firm hold on him stopped him from making a runner; the thought of the fox prowling around was still hanging at the back of his mind.

"Thank goodness, here you are!" Butterfly said. "Come this way, quickly! I've been looking for you everywhere!" he continued hurriedly without any other introduction.

Cockerel's vexed look met Rica's eyes.

"Do you know this butterfly?"

Rica didn't get to open his mouth and Butterfly spoke out:

"Follow me, quickly! I need your help!"

Rica was as baffled as his new friend, Cockerel: only a couple of hours ago cheeky Butterfly had been poking fun at him, and now he was begging for help. To Rica that looked like the perfect payback time:

"Let's get something straight, Butterfly, you might be colorful and cuddly, and a favorite with flowers, but if you are in trouble with Cuckoo or Magpie, that's not my fault. I told them nothing about you! There you have it!" Rica proclaimed convincingly.

Cockerel's eyes almost bulged out of their sockets.

"You know, Butterfly, I've told one too many lies today just to keep you safe, and for that reason alone, I think I deserve your respect..." Rica scolded remorsefully glaring at the sky.

"Have you been lying to me, too?" Cockerel asked quickly

"This is not a prank, I promise you," Butterfly hurried to reassure Rica. "It's about a sparrow chick..." Butterfly explained while gliding up and down on the wings of Wind.

"A sparrow chick? I haven't come across one of those today, sorry my friend!" Rica replied confused.

"No, no, what I meant to say is that a sparrow chick has fallen in water and he'll soon drown if we don't intervene!" Butterfly finally managed to make himself understood.

"So why are we standing here talking about it, let's just go there quickly!" Rica and Cockerel said in unison.

"This way, quickly!" Butterfly urged them.

Butterfly quickly mounted on Wind and in no time they were well on their way, with Rica and Cockerel following suit. Trying to make himself helpful, Wind grabbed Rica's quiff and started dragging him along. Fuelled by his own power alone, Cockerel fell behind and was rather gobsmacked to see Rica flying more than walking, his flat feet barely touching the ground.

"Hey, wait for me! That's not fair!" Cockerel called out, but to no avail.

The duckling had the main role to play in this adventure being the only one who could swim out and save the sparrow chick. Following the footpath, the party soon arrived at the nearby lake. The otherwise calm surface of the water was broken up by ripples coming from the spot where the sparrow chick was struggling to keep his head above the water; Butterfly had told them the truth!

The silence of the place was disturbed by the anguished calls of other sparrow chicks watching the horrifying scene from the safety of the nest built amongst the branches of a willow stretching over the lake. The still waters of the lake were slowly swallowing down the little chick. The promise of eternal peace in the midst of the blue deep lurked in the background like a merciless sentence, defying the suffering of those left behind.

Rica launched himself in the water with Butterfly hovering above his head. When they were almost halfway through, Cockerel finally reached the edge of the lake, out of breath and drenched in his own sweat. After a few seconds he could see Rica fishing the swallow chick out of the water and starting to make his way back to the shore. Just then a fierce pike cut in front of them:

"Not so fast, ducky-duck!" he disdainfully approached Rica. "Put that chick back in the water and leave nature take its course; you're meddling in things which are beyond you. The chick is meant for my lunch, and I'm determined to keep it that way!"

"For your lunch? I'm afraid you'll have to cancel your lunch arrangements, grandpa!" Rica replied tightening his hold on the chick. "This chick is coming with me!"

"The lake is rightfully mine, and so is everything that falls in it!" Pike claimed as his sharp teeth ground against each other with anticipation.

"I'm sure you'll get other things falling in your lake today, so why not let this one off!" Rica suggested.

"Or I can get two for one: swallow for lunch and duck for dinner!" Pike retorted menacingly.

As Pike opened his wide mouth, showing off his razor-sharp teeth, a stone landed in it causing Pike to sink to the bottom in the blink of an eye. A few froglets who were watching from the side, began to laugh, entertained by the turn of events. Pike hatefully glared at them which was enough to scare them off. Angry Pike spat out the stone together with a few teeth stuck into it, unable to understand what had happened.

Rica glanced to where the stone had come from and discovered Cockerel sizing up a few more stones, ready to continue the attack against Pike if needed.

"Get back to the shore as fast as you can, now!" he called out to Rica.

Rica was as speedy as he could, carrying his precious load, but he was only a little duck himself. From underneath the water, Pike kept an eye on the duckling's moving shadow; the chase was on again! Pike resurfaced and was met by the renewed artillery of Cockerel who was aiming quite accurately. But Pike was an old hand at hunting tactics and managed to avoid all stones by zigzagging in the waters of the lake. Pike came within inches from snapping Rica's tail, when the duckling hopped out of the water on a water lily pad. Pike nearly choked with spite.

"Enjoy your lily pad while it lasts… You are not on dry land yet!" he grinned.

"If you don't stop, I'll take you to court and you'll have to account for all you've done in front of Mr. Justice Crocodile!" Butterfly tried to distract him.

Pike couldn't believe what he was hearing:

"Are you threatening me in my own courtyard?" he smirked.

"It is your courtyard all right, but even there you have to follow the rules like everybody else!" Butterfly defied him again. "All those present heard you and will be witnesses during the trial!" he carried on aggravating Pike to give Rica a bit of time. Pike went underwater without saying anything else, and for a moment they all thought it was over.

"Good call on your part, Butterfly. Thank you for that!" Rica said. "It will all be just fine now!" he addressed the frightened swallow chick in a soothing voice.

But Rica had spoken too soon; the lily pad that hosted them began to tremble and shake and, without the intervention of Wind which quickly rebalanced him, he would have fallen into the lake again. Pike had his own plans: he had sunk back in the water, right to the bottom of the lake where the stalk of lily pads were soft and tender, and bit it off. He was now dragging the loose lily pad towards the middle of the lake where the waters ran deep and there was no vegetation growing above the surface. Wind intervened blowing as hard as he could in the opposite direction in an attempt to slow down to a halt the lily pad. But Pike was too strong a swimmer.

"Jump on another lily pad! Do it quickly while you still can!" Cockerel shouted in a state of panic.

But Rica was already making a huge effort to keep himself and the swallow where they were; gathering the strength to make the jump suddenly seemed an impossible task to him.

"I can't jump that far! It's simply too much!" he admitted realizing that another fall in the water would have been fatal for the rescued chick.

Without thinking twice about it, Cockerel ditched stone-throwing and nimbly hopped on the nearest lily pad, and then on another one and another one until he eventually reached close enough to the duckling.

"Throw the chick to me! Don't worry, I'll catch him!" he instructed Rica.

Rica did just that. As soon as Cockerel had the swallow chick in his arms, he made his way back to the shore, duly assisted by Wind which would rebalance him *after every jump. In no time, they were safe on dry land, with Rica following them from behind. Still under the water, Pike didn't know what to make of the lily pad which all of a sudden became light as a feather. By the time nasty Pike worked out what was going on, his lunch and dinner were out of reach.*

"Next time you won't get away so easily!" Pike shouted angrily, but nobody paid any attention to him.

Helpless and with no prospects for lunch or dinner, Pike examined the many holes in his teeth and couldn't refrain from feeling sorry for himself: Cockerel did such a good job of taking aim at his teeth, that Pike could consider himself lucky from then on if he had anything else but mushy seaweed for a meal. A gang of mosquitoes loitering on a lily pad were commenting on Pike's sad demise.

"Shame to leave such nice chicks get away! I wouldn't have minded a drop of their blood! You'd think an old pike like that had one or two tricks up his sleeve, but not this one..." they said laughingly.

Enough was enough for Pike: with a mighty blow of his tail, he raised a veil of water which swept the lot of mosquitoes off the lily pad. Once in the water, the mosquitoes became easy prey for a school of hatchlings swimming nearby.

"Save yourselves any way you can, brothers!" the one who had commented before urged his peers, but they had little or no hope of escaping and they knew it.

The sorry-looking Pike swam around despondently for a little while, just enough to catch a sight of the froglets who, safely sitting on a high rock, were having a good laugh at his failed attempt for bird-hunting.

In the meantime, both Rica and Cockerel carried the swallow chick further from water and checked his pulse. Seconds later the chick began to cough up water and after a short struggle his breath was back to normal, but the trauma of his experience soon came through as he started to weep and sob.

"You are safe now, no need to worry!" Rica spoke to him.

Acting upon a sixth sense that might have let them know that one of their chicks was in danger, the parent swallows flew back to the nest and were relieved to find their young one out of harm's way, if only very wet and scared. Mother Swallow carried a little basket skilfully weaved out of willow twigs, covered with a snow-white tea towel with an embroidered angel in each corner. She dropped the basket to open her arms wide for her chick who nestled next to her heart, half-expecting to be told off. Both parents kissed his forehead and hugged him warmly, knowing it was the only way to restore his confidence.

"There, there, dearest... the main thing is that you are well now!"

Next, the parents turned their attention to the other chicks in the nest who were chirping in distress.

"You stay right here, and I'll be back in no time!" Mother Swallow told her husband.

"Go and do what you must, and we'll be here when you return!" Father Swallow agreed.

Mother Swallow picked up the chick and flew up to the nest where she was welcomed with a choir of chirping by all the other chicks. She took off the scarf which she always wore around her neck and with swift and deft moves she wiped the water, the fear and the distress off her chick. It wasn't just any old scarf that she was wearing, but a magic one! She gently placed the chick back in the nest amongst all his siblings and cast a loving glance over them all. The oldest chick hurried to give her a complete account of events.

"The flower bud which we've been watching for a while blossomed up early this morning, just after you've left. The soft rustling noise drew our attention and our little brother got overly excited and started making his way to it before the rest of us could do anything. Before long, he stepped on tender twigs which couldn't take his weight and fell off in the water. We were all taken by surprise and didn't know what to do... Sorry about it!"

Mother Swallow looked each of them in the eye before she spoke:

"You must promise me that you'll be extra careful around water from here on... Water is no joke for the likes of us! This time we were lucky that these children happened to be playing nearby and could intervene, otherwise it doesn't even bear thinking about it!" she concluded kissing each of them on the forehead, thankful they were all safe and sound.

"Yes, Mom, we promise!" the chicks raised their small voices in a choir.

Peering at the four heroes underneath the willow tree, Mother Swallow had an idea:

"I know just the kind of thanks worthy of such brave youngsters!"

She disappeared in the nest where she stood in front of a red wooden cabinet with angels engraved on its front. It was hanging up on the wall and Mother Swallow opened it to get out a tiny box beautifully crafted out of willow twigs, with an oak leaf as a lid. Mother Swallow had it gifted by the Autumn Fairy who used to keep her blush in it.

She came back out and instructed her babies to stay out of trouble until she would be back.

"I can't thank you enough for your courage and kindness!" she said to Rica and his friends.

"Our pleasure, Mother Swallow!" Rica replied modestly. "It was a team effort and we couldn't have done it otherwise: without quick-thinking Butterfly who alerted us straight away, or without Cockerel saving the day at the last moment, I could have never succeeded!"

At that moment, Rica felt his quiff ruffled up and looking up he saw Wind gliding around with a grimace on his face.

"And I couldn't forget Wind, who was of great help, indeed!" Rica added hastily.

"Thank you all, a thousand times!" Mother Swallow took a bow in front of them.

Appeased by public recognition, Wind withdrew quietly on the side, near Butterfly.

"I can't even start to imagine what was in your mind when you decided to hop from lily pad to lily pad all the way to the middle of the lake and back. That was *something else..." Rica addressed Cockerel. They both stared at the rippling mirror of water where the water-lilies and the lily pads were still swaying slowly to and fro.*

Cockerel's comb went red. Caught in a storm of mixed emotions, he didn't know what to say: his intervention defied the laws of Physics, but deep down inside he felt an immense sense of pride.

Butterfly, on the other hand, had to admit that the duckling was full of surprises: humble and modest, he did not hesitate for one moment to share his victory with his friends, although he was, undoubtedly, the main hero of the rescue operation. He had proved thoughtful and considerate beforehand, when he got rid of Cuckoo for him by pointing him in the wrong direction. Butterfly did not say much, but he knew that Rica had won a special place in his heart.

Cockerel, however, bubbled up with pride hearing Rica's praise. He stood up so tall, that Rica had to put his head back to still be able to see his friend. Then he continued:

"To be perfectly honest, if it wasn't for Cockerel, I wouldn't be standing here now. Lucky, he thought of taking aim at Pike..."

"What do you mean he took aim at Pike?" Father Swallow asked getting puzzled, eyeing Cockerel up and down.

"Cockerel found some stones on the shore of the lake, took aim at Pike and struck him just as he was preparing to gobble us up; I was carrying your chick in my arms at the time..." Rica explained.

"You don't say!" Father Swallow marveled at such drama.

"That's right... and he had such good hand-eye coordination that the stone got right into Pike's open mouth and made him sink to the bottom of the lake because of the heavy weight..."

"And he was left without teeth... Ha-ha-ha!" Cockerel chuckled.

The grateful parents paid homage again to the rescuers for their courage:

"Words are not enough to express our gratitude. We'll make sure that word about your good deed will travel far and wide, until everybody knows about it. We'll both work tirelessly towards it from tomorrow onwards. You'll understand, I'm sure, that today will be taken up with restoring our chicks' confidence..." both parents announced.

"Of course, of course, you've got to look after your children first!" Rica answered reassuringly. "Wow… and are you really going to spread the word far and wide?" he repeated their words, his mind already racing to anticipate his sisters' reaction, hopeful that it might just be the kind of thing to finally endear him with them. Although he had won the respect of his friends, the only ones whose attention he truly wanted were still his sisters.

"Everyone will get to know about you, and that's a promise!" Father Swallow replied solemnly.

"It's a promise from me, too!" Mother Swallow pledged her support again.

Rica blushed with excitement and quickly slipped a glance towards his friends Cockerel and Butterfly… Wind was fluttering nearby, busying himself with dusting some pretty patterns on Butterfly's wings, but still paying close attention to *everything going on around; always on the move, always roaming from one place to another, staying true to his nature...*

Rica, Cockerel, Butterfly and Wind... so different, yet so well teamed up on the day! They were all happy and content to be part of the mix.

"*Every deed has its rightful payment in this world, and today you've proved yourselves selfless and brave by saving a young life! Life is valuable at any age, and you've put yourselves on the line to make provision for a perfect stranger. That cannot go unrewarded!*"

Coming from a swallow, which legend has it, stands for purity of heart and noble thought, those words made a big impression on the four friends. Moreover, the unexpected promise of a reward contributed to the many surprises which kept producing themselves out of the blue on that day.

"My gift to each of you is a beauty spot!" Mother Swallow chirped cheerfully. The four friends looked at one another in surprise.

"Yes, yes, I know, it's not a gift you'd expect every day… Besides, it's not the kind of beauty spot that speckled hens got! Not at all! Those sly sisters got their speckles by dint of craftiness. We got the beauty spots you will be gifted with by divine blessing and hard work," she assured them, guiding their eyes towards Father Swallow's beauty spot, a burgundy little dot which lit up his handsome face. "Your beauty spots will bring up your natural beauty even more, like the stars beautify the velvety night sky, and they always hold the promise of fulfilment in life!"

Wise words usually hold a grain of truth, and Mother Swallows were no exception: the beauty spots she had to give away as she pleased, had been picked by

herself and her husband from the shimmering surface of the ocean, at a mysterious time of twilight when falling stars take their bath in the living waters on earth. The noble nature of swallows ideally combines resilience and a light touch, which makes them the perfect beauty-spot pickers. All the effort they put in their long flights and the care they employ to crop the divine gifts are well worth it: the beauty spots are life-long lucky charms, an endless source of energy for their owners and a sign of good fortune and great achievements throughout life."

I was lying on the bed, drinking in every one of my mother's words and at that point in the story, I involuntarily reached out and touched one of the beauty spots on her cheek. My mom smiled kindly; she knew exactly what I was thinking. The many beauty spots on her face must have been a sign of a good nature, as well as of a good fortune! She reached out in return and caressed my head. She understood there was no chance she could put us to bed before she finished the story.

"Rica, Butterfly, Wind, and Cockerel felt a warm glow in their tummies and nearly stopped breathing… the exhilaration of the moment made their hearts throb in their little chests… Aware of their state of mind, Mother Swallow opened the box with deft moves and a blinding glow filled the air around. The four friends had to cover their eyes for a moment and give themselves a chance to adjust to the new light. When they finally managed to regain their acuity, they all stepped closer and took a look in the little, red box that Mother Swallow held in her hand: a lot of star-shaped droplets rested on the bottom of the box, glowing as bright as the stars in the sky on a clear summer's night. The dainty box had them all orderly sat against a navy, velvet ground which drew in the eyes of the on-lookers like a miniature universe.

"I can tell you now that the four friends were mesmerized watching the wonderful show of shimmer, glow and color which unraveled in front of their eyes, just like you are watching me with your little mouths wide open, ready to sip in the rest of the story," Mom teased us all, smiling.

"Mother Swallow picked up one of the starry droplets and, with solemn and slow ritual movements, approached Rica. The starlet in her beak beaconed an even brighter light as if to rise to the importance of the moment.

"I gift this to you with a grateful heart for your bravery which saved my child's life today! Your beauty spot will be part of you from now on, flesh of your flesh fed by your own blood!" the swallow told him in a soft voice gently placing the beauty spot on his right cheek.

Rica felt a shiver running up and down his spine," Mom explained staring into my eyes.

I took advantage of the brief pause in Mom's story to release the air I had been holding in for a while, as I could hardly bring myself to breathe in case I would miss out on something. Mom's eyes were resting on the beauty spot on my right cheek and for some reason I felt the place suddenly caressed by a warm breeze. I touched my spot and from that moment on I knew it was my signature feature, my lucky charm.

"Did Mother Swallow place the beauty spot on his right cheek?" I asked eagerly.

"She did, indeed!" Mom confirmed my thoughts with a wink.

My sisters started wising up to Mom's story in the meantime, exchanging meaningful glances amongst themselves.

"Mother Swallow came to each of them in turn and performed the same ritual as she passed on to them the precious gifts. Thus, Cockerel, then Butterfly and Wind received their well-deserved reward. Each beauty spot perfectly fitted their new owners in size, color, and shape: Rica's and Cockerel's were slightly bigger than Butterfly's. Some of the flowers which witnessed the ceremony from the side bobbed their heads invitingly towards the lucky Butterfly: the dewdrops on their petals could be as many mirrors in which he could admire his new look. Others, turned their heads to the sun, unwilling to have anyone spoiling their complicated hairdos.

Wind glided quickly across the lawn to the shore of the lake to have a good look at his new appearance, but when he stared in the still waters of the lake all he could see was a hideous face with a smirk on it. He jumped back thinking that Mother Swallow's gift spoilt his good looks, but when he went back to see his reflection again, he realized that Pike had been spying on them all along from underneath the surface of the water. Caught in the act, he was now withdrawing at a speed behind some boulders at the bottom of the lake. Wind did his best to blow the surface water as hard as he could, but his limited strength only succeeded to send ripples to the middle of the lake where they got swallowed into the depth. Wind rejoined his friends who were admiring one another, very pleased with their gifts.

Mother Swallow beamed with joy herself seeing how much they appreciated the gifts.

"Your beauty spots will stick to your cheeks forever, becoming part of who you are as soon as somebody who loves you gives you a hug and a kiss."

"Beg your pardon?" the four friends said in unison.

"Yes, you heard me: a warm and genuine expression of love will make them stick and stay there forever. Warm and genuine love, just like your reaction today!" Mother Swallow emphasized.

Their first thought was that they were too young to have experienced love! Would they have to wait for years until their precious gifts could become theirs at last? But almost instantly they realized that love is of many kinds, and the one love they had known from birth was their family's love for them.

"This is not just any gift which you unwrap and play with to your heart's content, only to throw it in a corner when you've had enough of it! A beauty spot is a divine blessing meant to shine a light on your destiny and as the living proof of a divine

blessing it will give you the guiding wisdom that will help you conquer any hardship, but your thoughts, acts, and emotions will have to always provide the positive energy which keeps it active, if not, you risk losing it!"

The four friends looked each other in the eyes and said nothing.

The beauty spots on their cheeks could already connect to their emotions: the uncertainty in their hearts was soon picked up and translated as a slight tremor at the point of contact with the spot. A few sun rays roaming around sneaked their way down through the branches of the willow tree and, mistaking their beauty spots for dew drops, got themselves ready to fizzle them up into little steam clouds. Always vigilant, Mother Swallow blocked their way by shading the heroes of the day with one of her wings.

"Shoo away, it's not what you think it is!" she urged the sunrays, who stopped in their tracks and changed direction.

"My dear children, what you have to keep in mind from now on is never to give in to sadness, worry, and sorrow, because they are the greatest threats to the well-being of your beauty spots. You can lose your beauty spots to any one of those three evils!"

"Lose our beauty spots?" Rica, Cockerel and Butterfly protested at the same time.

"I'm not saying that you will, just warning you that beauty spots don't have long lives when placed on the cheeks of sadness, worry and sorrow."

"But our beauty spots are on OUR cheeks!" the three children struggled to make sense of Mother Swallow's warning.

At that moment, Wind, who had understood what Mother Swallow meant, swept in front of them and stroked their faces.

"Wind is right!" Mother Swallow welcomed Wind's well-timed intervention. "We can all sense the wind by feeling his movement on our bodies, or by smelling the occasional fragrance which it may carry, but we never really see it!"

"So, what you are saying is that sadness, worry, and sorrow do the same?" Rica started to work it out for himself.

"That's right, young drake, sadness, worry and sorrow take on the face of those who host them in their hearts! And they are not as nice and friendly as Wind! These insidious enemies of happiness not only kill the joy of life in all those who are gullible enough to welcome them, but they also cause beauty spots to wither and die, as well!"

The children finally understood what Mother Swallow wanted to get across: once you surrender to sadness, worry, and sorrow, you lose ownership of your body and mind, and therefore, you lose your beauty spot!

"Always remember to be happy and cheerful and never to give in to grumpy moods! Keep in mind that all beauty spots are star dust fallen from heaven and they

can only exist in surroundings which is very much alike with their home grounds: thus, the purity of heart, the joy of life and happy thoughts are what you must indulge in from here on."

Butterfly chuckled to himself: happiness was as close to him as his own skin, so he had nothing to worry about. Rica, on the other hand, had a consistent companion in sadness every time his sisters rejected or ignored him; he asked with tears in his voice:

"So, could I lose my beauty spot at some point?"

"I'm afraid so, my dear child… Beauty spots are like grafts to trees: they get fed the energy which flows through their host's body, and that means that the end-result can go either way. A beauty spot is the mark of Divinity on an earthling's face, and they can only live in perfect harmony with those who reflect the divine in the way they live their lives. Whether you'll be able to keep your gift, or not, depends entirely on yourselves!"

The four friends checked one another out with questioning eyes: would they be able to rise to that sort of challenge? But it was not enough time to overthink things! Impatient chirping broke out of the nest hidden amongst the branches of the willows.

"I have to go now but thank you again for everything and good luck!" Mother Swallow greeted the four little heroes before she flew to her nest. It was feeding time for the baby birds and a busy time for Mother and Father Swallow.

The four friends were left to chew on their thoughts. Wind was frolicking around, trying to take their minds off grim thoughts by telling them about Pike spying on them from the water. Butterfly was the only one who could work out what he meant; luckily, Pike was of no consequence to them anymore.

The four of them decided it was time to go and leave in peace the family of swallows who had been through a lot that day. They had their thanks, the reward they had received exceeded all expectations and it was now time to depart the scene!

As soon as they were on their way, Butterfly started dancing around Rica and eventually let himself crash land right in the middle of his quiff for a laugh,

"You still haven't told me why you've wandered away from home on your own. You are a long way away now and a lot of things can happen to a little duckling walking on his own…" he challenged Rica.

"I left home in search for a friend!" Rica confessed.

Butterfly flew off and settled again on Rica's beak, so he could see his eyes.

"Are you an orphan?" Cockerel asked quickly.

Cockerel also stopped suddenly from his brisk walk, so that he could face Rica. His shadow jumped over from behind him, brought to a sudden standstill.

"Of course not, I'm not an orphan!" replied Rica surprised at such an idea. His quiff swayed to and fro in a funny way, much to Butterfly's delight.

"But enough with you questioning me," Rica turned to Butterfly, "I think it's about time you tell me more about yourself... you've been asking questions since we first bumped into each other, but you've never given away anything about yourself... and to think that I had to lie for you earlier!" Rica mumbled recalling his conversation with Cuckoo.

"You have my eternal gratitude for that!" Butterfly thanked him. "I've been asking you lots of questions because I saw you wandering on your own, all sad and

lonely. You might know that we butterflies have a duty of care to try and lift the spirits of all those who experience sorrow in any way, shape or form. No offence meant, but you looked like a classic case…"

Wind was drawing circles around Butterfly with the obvious intention of communicating something. Butterfly turned his attention to him for a moment, then shook his head in disagreement. But Wind insisted, and with Rica and Cockerel watching perplexed from the other side, Butterfly eventually conceded:

"OK, OK," he said appealingly.

"What is your friend saying?" Rica asked.

"He wants me to tell you that all butterflies share a certain gift…" he explained a bit embarrassed.

"What is that?" it was their turn to eagerly ask questions.

"It's more like a skill we are born with…"

"A gift, a skill, whatever… Will you tell us what it is and stop taking us for a pair of dummies?" Rica grumbled grumpily.

"It's enough for us to show up somewhere… anywhere…" Butterfly was taking his time explaining.

"Oh, brother … Will you spill the beans already?" Rica and Cockerel burst out impatiently.

"Here is the thing: it's enough for us, butterflies to show up somewhere, and sadness vanishes away from that place!" Butterfly confessed.

"Are you saying that you guys can cheer up all beasts, whether it's a lion, a jackal, wolf, fox, or even a crow?" Cockerel tried to make sense of the new revelation they'd been let into.

"Right you are!" Butterfly confirmed in a crystal-clear voice.

"This is like… like… like keeping company with the Holy Spirit at all times!" Cockerel struggled for the right wording.

"I couldn't have put it better myself!" Butterfly agreed with him immediately, returning his smile, while Wind rushed to the side and applauded approvingly. "But I have to admit that I had trouble working my magic on you, so I decided to go to your house and see for myself the source of all the upset!" Butterfly informed him.

"You did that!" Rica raised his eyebrows in surprise.

"And what have you found there?" Cockerel couldn't help asking straight away.

"Let's say just say that it was… very interesting: an awful lot of girls in your household!" he turned his attention to Rica again. "And they all looked like you!"

At that point, Wind started blowing this way and that way around Butterfly, trying to draw his attention:

"What's the problem?" Butterfly asked him quietly.

Wind implored for Butterfly's discretion: wandering in and out of Rica's house without being invited was an act of intrusion, and he felt embarrassed of it. Butterfly blinked quickly to let Wind know that his secret was safe with him, then continued to address Rica:

"The girls were modelling in front of an audience made up of ants and little bugs..."

"Yup, they were definitely my sisters!" Rica agreed.

"So, you've got sisters... a lot of them, as well!" Cockerel smiled happy for his friend.

"Very many..." Butterfly emphasized.

"How can you be sad when you are surrounded by so many siblings?" Cockerel couldn't quite understand. Mother Swallow's words were still lingering on at the back of his mind, and he worried terribly that Rica, in a right state as he was, risked losing his beauty spot.

Rica cast him a glance and said nothing. Butterfly came to the rescue.

"The truth is that the insects were paying little, or no attention to your sisters, except for those who had something to gain from it!" The irony in Butterfly's voice did not go unnoticed. Rica looked at him skeptically, not knowing what to think of it, but Wind was nodding approvingly while going round and round his friends.

"Aren't you lucky to belong to such a big family?" Cockerel declared admiringly, ignoring Butterfly's comments.

"Lucky! Are you serious? If anything, I'd call this tough luck!" Rica retorted gloomily.

"Well, it's common knowledge that love is not in short supply within large families; look at the sun which gives life to the world around us: love is really and truly in the air!" Cockerel declared flicking his comb from one side to the other, making it turn all crimson with excitement.

Butterfly couldn't believe his eyes: how did Cockerel manage to pull out that clever trick just like that!

"I should be so lucky!" Rica replied in a desolate voice. "If that was the case, why would I choose to leave home in search for a friend, and why would I be here with you now, telling you the ins and outs of my sad story?"

"I think I know where you are going with this; your sisters must be some right madams, are they not?" Cockerel had it all worked out.

"You can say that again!" Rica agreed with Cockerel's take on the situation.

He sighed heavily, and Wind rushed to seize steamy breath and turned it into a heart-shaped cloud which he then attached on Rica's chest as a badge, in an attempt to raise his spirits. But Rica was not in the mood for any of it, and with a wave of his wing made the fluffy heart vanish in the air, which left Wind rather disappointed.

"What a shame!" Butterfly muttered to himself.

Burdened and with his head lowered down, Rica started walking again. How could anyone ever understand his sorrow? Coming from such a large family should *have made things better, not worse. Cockerel soon caught up with Rica, matching his pace of walk with that of the duckling's. Their shadows moving together at the same pace seemed to have locked arms in friendship!*

"What bothers me the most is the fact that they act as if I don't even exist. There's nothing I wouldn't do to please them, but nothing of what I do is good enough for them!"

"I'm sure it's not that bad!" Cockerel consoled him. "After all, you are their little brother, their only brother… Surely you must mean a lot to them!"

"If it were as you say, would they have let me leave home on my own? I even warned them that I was going to wander off, but they didn't even hear me!" Rica explained sorrowfully. "I bet all my pocket money that they haven't notice my absence at all!"

Cockerel turned around in the middle of the road and stood still in front of Rica, blocking his way forward. Rica stopped abruptly vexed by his friend's gesture.

"I'm sure it's not as bad as it seems!" he declared in a cheerful voice.

"What do you mean?" Rica questioned.

"Your sisters must have been very busy, indeed, that's why they haven't noticed your departure!" he replied triumphantly, happy to find a plausible explanation.

Wind was snaking this way and that way, agreeing with everything Cockerel said and hoping to eventually appease the duckling.

"They seem like a bunch of silly little girls, more interested in showing off their catwalk than anything else! It's not that they have anything against you, they are too engrossed in play to pay attention to anyone or anything else."

"Do you really think that?" Rica's hopes started to rise again.

"I know that," with every word Cockerel became more confident in his opinion. "You said you could bet all your pocket money that they haven't noticed you missing after all this time!"

"That's always been a problem for me, and now you are saying it's the solution! I don't get it! "Rica replied in a strop.

Cockerel was ready for a long explanation, but Rica had already set out on his way, more upset than ever. He slipped a glance towards Butterfly who was gliding above him. He knew what he meant; the girls in Rica's family had lived in their own little world to which Rica was an outcast!

Butterfly dropped back and let Rica march on his own for a while. With swift and definitive gestures, he made Cockerel understand that questioning Rica any further would do him more harm than good.

Rica waddled briskly until most of his anger had vented off, then he slowed down to let his friends catch up with him. As soon as Cockerel was walking shoulder to shoulder with him again, it was his turn to ask some questions:

"What about you? What are you doing wandering around on your own? Good thing I found you when I did, otherwise you could have ended up as someone's dinner as you were lying there senseless..." Rica held back from mentioning the fox again.

Cockerel looked Rica in the eye: he had the feeling that the duckling was mature beyond his age, or perhaps loneliness and sadness wised him up to the world around sooner than usual!

"I was in search of a friend, very much like you!" he explained.

Rica stopped; he didn't expect that Cockerel stopped next to him.

"Are you going through the same thing as me?" Rica asked, moved.

"I wish I were!" Cockerel's mood dulled becoming more like Rica's.

"But you said..." Rica was totally confused.

"Are you an orphan?" Butterfly intervened from above where he was giving Wind a ride for a change.

Rica watched the two of them in shock; that thought never crossed his mind. Cockerel was well presented, decently dressed, and well-fed for an orphan.

"No, I'm not an orphan!" he denied sadly.

"Then what's your reason for upset?" Rica insisted.

"Out of all my family, only granddad and I are still around. He is so old, that he can hardly walk..." Cockerel opened up.

"What happened to the rest of your family?" Rica couldn't stop asking questions.

Cockerel stared at his friends and swallowed hard before he could continue.

"Yes, where are your parents, brothers, and sisters?" Butterfly tried hard to grasp some logical explanation.

"I've lost them all..." Cockerel had tears in his voice.

"How?" the two were gobsmacked.

"To some old foxes who go hunting around here! My family had received an invitation to an anniversary from some relatives who lived over the other side of the Dock-Leaf Valley. My family was attacked while crossing through the valley... I'm not sure whether you are familiar with the place..." he commented hoping that at least Wind would have known what he was talking about.

"I know it!" Wind confirmed with a nod of the head.

"Have they left you behind on the day?" Rica guessed.

"Kind of... I keep telling myself that it was God's will... or else I would have ended up like the rest of my family..."

"Why weren't you with them?" Rica urged him to tell the story.

"They left me home with granddad..."

"Oh, sorry to hear that!" Rica muttered.

"Don't be... If they had taken me with them, I wouldn't have been here today talking to you!"

"I meant: sorry to hear about what happened to your family," Rica explained himself.

Wind decided it had been enough messing around and descended from Butterfly's back where he'd been enjoying a good old ride. They looked at each other and both of them agreed silently that Rica and Cockerel should be made aware how lucky they were to have their wishes come true.

"I think we all agree that we've heard enough sad stories to last us a year, and now we should focus on happier things happening in our lives: for instance, the two of you have just had your wish come true!" Butterfly called out as Wind had asked him to.

Rica and Cockerel looked puzzled at each other.

"What wish?" they quipped at the same time.

"You both have made a friend in each other! Considering that only this morning you've set out looking for a friend, that's pretty good going, don't you think?" Butterfly pointed out. Rica and Cockerel's eyes met again.

"You have got to be kidding me: you look around as if you have no idea what I'm talking about! I'm telling you: you've become good friends and you've saved a life in the process! That's no small thing, believe me!" Butterfly went on and on excitedly.

"But we've become good friends with you and Wind, for that matter, and what life-saving thing are you talking about?" Cockerel interrupted his tirade.

"My goodness, and I thought I had a short memory! I'm talking about the baby swallow who almost drowned this morning!" Butterfly reminded him.

With the truth of Butterfly's words fully dawning on them, Rica and Cockerel fell at a loss of words. In fact, they all felt like having a big hug to seal their newly born friendship. As Cockerel rushed to cuddle Rica, and Wind swept off to do the same for his friend, Butterfly, the latter gave a fearful scream which froze everybody in their positions. Thinking it was his fault, Wind sat himself quietly on a boulder at the side of the road and kept still for a few moments."

"What was wrong with Butterfly?" I hurriedly asked Mom, in fear that something terrible happened to the ever-cheerful hero in her story.

"Butterfly caught sight of his own reflection in the tears of joy on Wind's face," Mom filled me in, "and he saw something which gave him a great scare!"

"What's the matter? Has anything happened to you?" Rica and Cockerel enquired baffled.

Butterfly held his face and replied in a low, tearful voice:

"My starry dewdrop which Mother Swallow gave me…"

"What about that?" Rica and Cockerel still didn't understand.

"It's gone!" Butterfly cried.

In an instant, Rica and Cockerel felt their cheeks, only to face the disappointment of not being able to find their beauty spots, either. Alerted in this most dramatic way, Wind rushed to the first dewdrop he could find on a flower petal and stared at his reflection: his beauty spot had disappeared as well! Panic-stricken, they fell on their knees searching every single inch of land, like hounds haul in the game. They even traced back their steps until they reached the willow tree with the swallow nest. All their efforts came to nothing! Desperate, they looked up at the nest where the swallow family was chatting with a swarm of small insects. The children were the first to notice them and alerted their parents:

"Mom and Dad, the four children who saved our brother earlier today are here again!"

"Look after one another and I'll be back in a jiffy!" Mother Swallow called out. Then both parents flew to the ground.

"What brings you back so soon?"

In a state of shock and talking over each other, the four children gave a detailed account on how they realized soon after they left the place that their beauty spots have disappeared! Finally making head and tail of their chaotic explanations, Mother Swallow calmed them down with a broad smile and a chuckle. The four friends couldn't understand anything anymore.

"It's a good sign!" Mother Swallow dispelled their fears. "It means that your bodies have accepted and taken ownership of the beauty spots, like the ground swallows up a seed only to enable it to sprout and give out new life!"

"Are the beauty spots not lost, then? Will they show up on our faces again?" Rica lit up hearing what Mother Swallow had to say as he touched the place where the beauty spot had been planted earlier that day.

"Just remember what I told you: your beauty spot will be activated by a heart-warming hug and a kiss from somebody who truly loves you!" Mother Swallow drew on what she had told them before.

"What if some of us don't have anyone who cares about them to that extent?" Cockerel wanted to know. "What will happen then?"

Mother Swallow turned to him and thought for a few moments. Her heart went out to him as she instantly grasped the meaning behind Cockerel's unsettling inquiring.

"Those who don't have anyone to love them to that extent, will have to work hard and make somebody love them and cherish them."

The four friends looked at one another and smiled full of hope.

"The magic of a beauty spot starts with its coming into being and continues forever after; if you don't have a family, you seek out those who can become your family, you make them your friends, you grow together and help each other become better and greater than ever before..."

"How can you make somebody love you and miss you when you are not there?"
Rica felt silly asking that question.

"In order to make somebody love you, you have to love them first. When you love someone, you put them first and do the best you can for them. It's the way love works its magic in this world: in order to get, you have to give first, not knowing if the other person will eventually love you back, but that's a risk we all have to take!"
Mother Swallow put them in the picture.

With Mother Swallow's message still sinking in, the four children couldn't help feeling that they had let themselves down a bit: had they taken in Mother Swallow's advice the first time around, they wouldn't have been so easily led into a state of panic. But doubt is the mother of learning in all circumstances, and they all felt they had come out of the experience with renewed strength and more determination than ever.

"Be safe on your way, dear children, and always have faith in your guiding star that watches over you day and night; even when you can't see it, it can still see you from high above!" Mother Swallow bid them goodbye.

Rica, Cockerel, Butterfly and Wind set out in the same direction for the second time that day, after quickly peeking in the waters of the lake, checking if Pike was still hanging around. But the trouble-maker was nowhere to be seen.

Finding himself at a bit of a loose end, Butterfly started doing what he always did when he had a bit of time to himself, which was singing. That put a smile on Cockerel's face, who turned to him to ask:

"How did you two run into each other?" he pointed his chin at Rica and Butterfly.

"I accidentally bumped into him while roaming around, just before meeting you!" Butterfly duly informed him.

"You don't say!" Cockerel seemed surprised. "So, the two of you only met today?!"

"Yes, why is that such a big deal?" Butterfly retorted in his turn.

"No big deal! You two act as if you've known each other for years, that's all!" Cockerel made the point.

"We do?" Butterfly had never thought of it that way.

"Yup," Cockerel confirmed while thinking that actually, in his heart, he felt like he knew his new friends forever, too.

Rica walked on absent-mindedly, and Butterfly took upon himself to retell the story of their encounter to Cockerel.

"It all started in the morning after paying my usual visit to my favorite flower bud. When I first spotted it randomly and I touched down on it, I sensed the miracle of a little heartbeat and I knew I had to come back again and again, nurse it and look after it, if ever there was a need for it. "

"Seriously?" Rica interrupted, finally moving his stare from the ground to Butterfly who was dancing just above them in the air.

"Of course, this is serious stuff, what do you think!" Butterfly told Rica off for doubting him. Rica lowered his eyes again, taking notice as he did so to the little buzzing bugs looking after the newly sprouted buds.

"If it's not too much to ask, can you introduce us to it one day?" Rica interfered again.

"Who's it!" always distracted by the tiniest detail, Butterfly got caught unaware.

"Your flowerbud!" Rica put him back on the right track.

"Oh, yes, of course, it's a pretty flower with twelve petals altogether!" Butterfly said lovingly.

"Why no more, or no less than twelve petals?" Cockerel's interest suddenly raised by facts and figures.

"This flower produces twelve petals exactly because it sheds one petal for every month of the year, as a way of celebrating the change of seasons in nature."

"It means that your flower keeps up all round the year. By what you are saying I'm guessing it is a species of fir tree."

"Not at all, I'm talking about petals, not about spiky leaves. Besides, the fir tree leaves are already well used in nature: there is always a back to scratch, or some fur to untangle..."

Butterfly did not give away much. Wind nodded approvingly thinking of the many occasions when he used the leaves of a fir tree to pin together his mane, or to play darts with his friends.

"And what kind of flower is it?" Cockerel insisted. "Or is this a butterfly-style mystery?"

"Even if I wanted to, I couldn't keep secrets from my friends: it's a lotus flower!"

Rica and Cockerel looked at each other questioningly; they had never heard of such a flower before.

"But how is it possible that a flower shed one petal every month, throughout the four seasons which, in turn, bring life and death for the nature around...?"

"Ancient Wind is the master and orchestrator of the entire process. He helps the lotus flower shed one petal at a time and carries it himself on the shrine of each month..."

"But every flower is meant to live their life within a certain season, not around the year!" Rica protested.

"That's very simple to understand: the bud sprouts into a flower, and Ancient Wind takes care of the rest... the great mysteries of nature!" Butterfly summed it up.

His account made sense, especially considering that Wind confirmed every bit of it; in a nutshell, it was the cycle of a tender bud turning into a beautiful flower.

"Ancient Wind takes them on his wings to the four corners of the earth. Every time a petal falls off, Ancient Wind is there to catch it and ferry it around the world until he sees it safely reaching its destination!" Butterfly went on.

"What is the final destination?" Rica became curious, being himself a great lover of the stories on the Ancient Wind which his grandparents used to recount to him.

"No one knows exactly where Ancient Wind stores its treasures. He is the steward which holds the keys of the safest life banks in the universe, and legend has it that all forms of life are sampled there and put into safe-keeping until it's time for them to become useful and sprout new life..." Butterfly put on an air of wisdom while lecturing his friends about the ways of Ancient Wind.

"Ancient Wind is a very interesting character, he really is, and so is the way you nurture your favorite flowerbud to help it sprout into a special and beautiful flower, but I have to say that it's all too emotionally charged for me..." Cockerel confessed.

"I don't only nurture my favorite flowerbud to become the best flower it can be, I nurture all the plants around and help them become their best. Working in harmony with Mother-Nature is the meaning of my life!" Butterfly made it clear for Cockerel.

"OK, if you say so!" Cockerel conceded.

"It's not only me saying, Cockerel, in fact, what I've just told you will come to pass whether I say it, or not!" Butterfly made it clear.

"All right, all right, you work in harmony with Mother-Nature at all times, I understand that, but here is something I struggle to understand: how come that a butterfly is best friends with a duckling? You don't see that happening very often in nature; an insect and a bird bonded by a beautiful friendship! I would really like to find out more about that story! Do you mind?"

"Not at all, I'll be happy to oblige!" Butterfly replied, happy to carry on being the center of attention. Wind settled down for a while nearby, ready to listen as well.

"As I was saying, just after I called on my flowerbud this morning, as I was casually fluttering around, I happened to see this… young drake," Butterfly began his story as he flew around a few times before he sat himself on Rica's quiff. "He was wandering around all alone!"

"I first spotted you as a strange extension in the projection of my shadow!" Rica remembered with a faint smile.

"You were very upset and talking to yourself," Butterfly reminded him. Wind who was quietly gliding by, became suddenly interested and eager to say something.

"Wind says that all his peers going back and forth warned each other about you: the general idea was to avoid making contact with you…" Butterfly interpreted Wind's account of events.

"His peers avoided making contact with me?" Rica repeated baffled.

"That's what Wind says!" Butterfly confirmed.

"Why were they avoiding me?" Rica asked.

"Sadness and sorrow are easily spread around and no breeze or gust of wind would want to catch any of these pests!" Butterfly translated again for Wind.

"Is that even possible? Can somebody come down with sadness and sorrow, like you do with a disease?" Rica seemed unconvinced.

"Of course, it's possible!" Butterfly spoke for himself this time, "All you need is to come in brief contact with somebody who is sad, and you've got it next!"

"Just as simple as that?" Cockerel intervened.

"Just like that: sadness, dirt, disease can spread like wild fire if you don't watch them closely…" Butterfly continued.

Cockerel kept his eyes on him, still doubtful.

"High temperature, low temperature, cold, flu, allergy, lethargy, you can catch them all before you know it, if you are not careful!" Butterfly got carried away with himself.

"Allergy and lethargy, what are those things?" Cockerel muttered under his breath confused.

"Yes, you can!" Butterfly emphasized making sure there was no doubt left in Cockerel's mind about the seriousness of the situation.

"Oh, boy, first my sisters didn't want anything to do with me, and then breezes and gusts are taking the long way around rather than come in contact with me… this is spreading fast, Wind is quite right!"

Rica was itching to change the topic as soon as possible, before he got himself into a muddle and started thinking of Wind as his enemy, rather than his friend. More sensitive and empathetic by nature, Butterfly nodded his head in the direction of Wind wishing to thank him for his intervention, while secretly hoping to bring it to an end. Wind accepted his tacit suggestion and took it as a compliment, unaware of the unease of his friends, and rather proud of himself.

"I was glad to have you pop up in my way!" Butterfly reassured Rica.

"Were you? Really?" the duckling cheered up.

"You bet I was!" Butterfly played along.

"But how could you be glad? You are bubbly and happy all the time, and you like being in the company of others like you!" Rica replied confused, but still hopeful.

"I like to be with those who need me!" Butterfly corrected him, slightly frowning at Wind who was blowing his wings on and off, to create a hypnotic ripple of velvety color gleaming in the sunshine. But he knew that, after all, it was only an innocent game, so he lit up. It was not in his nature to stay grumpy for too long.

"What made you think I needed you?" Rica was happy to have raised someone's attention after all.

"You were glum and morose, not even looking where you were going." Butterfly shrugged his shoulders, implying that it was not much more to say about it.

"And what happened next?" Cockerel took up on Butterfly's hint and tried to speed up the pace.

"I rested on his back and fluttered my wings up and down, so that his shadow looked like an angel! It was my way of getting his attention!" Butterfly commented.

"I didn't know anyone can do that!" Cockerel made an effort to imagine the scene but wasn't very successful.

"I'd rather show this to you, than explain it! Words don't do it justice!" Butterfly replied as he flew off and then landed on Cockerel's back where he started flapping his wings up and down.

"Now have a look at your own shadow!" he urged Cockerel who watched mesmerized the two shadows merging to produce the shape of an angel.

"I'm an angel, I'm an angel, everybody look at me!" he exclaimed excitedly.

He looked up in the air, still in disbelief that he was seeing his own shadow, and much more inclined to expect a real angel hovering above him.

"Did you get the duckling's attention?" Cockerel got the story back on track.

"I did, but unfortunately it was the wrong kind of attention; the duckling got uppity with me and acted offended!" Butterfly said, still unable to understand how it all went so wrong.

"Did you get uppity with him for doing that?" Cockerel questioned Rica, perplexed at his reaction.

Rica kept quiet. Only a heavy sigh came out instead, and Wind hurried to seize the steamy breath and model it into the shape of a heart which he attached on Cockerel's chest as a token of his friendship with Rica. Cockerel felt like touching it, but Wind urged him not to. Cockerel stood still, not daring to lift a finger for fear that the beautiful wispy heart would just vanish into thin air.

"To make a long story short, the duckling was very upset and all my attempts to cheer him up led to nothing, so I decided to investigate on my own the cause of his upset."

Wind rushed around in protest.

"Sorry, wrong choice of words, WE decided to investigate, my friend Wind and I!" Butterfly rephrased. Wind slithered along appeased by the amends of Butterfly.

"We were soon on our way to find duckling's home and let the family know of his whereabouts."

"Did you find the house?" Cockerel wanted to know.

"Yes, that was the easy part!"

"And then?"

"We didn't have much success in getting the girls' attention, either!"

"What do you mean by that?" Cockerel wanted details.

"The girls were still busy doing the catwalk…" Butterfly informed him.

"Was there a cat while they were doing their walk? Are they OK?" Rica plunged into a state of panic.

"Calm down, young drake, they are fine, a catwalk is a fashion show, the kind of thing that your sisters spend hours doing!"

"It's all right, then!" Rica sighed with relief.

"So, what was the problem with that?" Cockerel insisted.

"There was no problem, but I didn't get much of a look in, that's all!"

"No way!" the others couldn't quite believe it.

Wind, in the meantime, became disgruntled again and started fussing around.

"Correction, we didn't get much of a look in!" Butterfly came back on himself, but cast a reproachful glance towards his friend who was not very happy with him that day.

"I can't believe they even ignored guests!" Rica burst out annoyed.

"They didn't do it out of nastiness, it was just too much going on around: a catwalk, a fashion show and so on, and so forth," Butterfly argued their side.

"See? What did I tell you! Now, do you believe me? They are so engrossed in their own little thing, that they can't be bothered about anything or anyone else!" Rica flapped his wings, finally happy to have his argument confirmed.

"Were the parents at home?" Cockerel asked.

"They weren't, but what I saw was enough for me to understand the cause of duckling's upset, so I flew back to find you and keep you company!" Butterfly quipped merrily.

"Did you come back for me?" Rica's heart melted at the thought that somebody did care for him that much.

Butterfly noticed his change in mood and felt he was getting somewhere with the little sad duckling.

"When I arrived at the spot where I had left you, however, you were nowhere to be found, as if you had vanished into thin air, touch wood!" Butterfly explained.

"What's touching wood got to do with anything?" Cockerel seemed surprised at Butterfly's funny use of words.

"You say 'touch wood' when you mention something scary which you hope won't happen," Butterfly filled in Cockerel.

"Like what?" Cockerel still couldn't follow the argument.

"Like the thought of duckling vanishing into thin air!" Butterfly returned to the conversation going on beforehand.

"Why would a thought be scary? A thought is just a thought, there's nothing to it!" Cockerel had difficulty making sense of it.

"My dear friend, there is a lot more to thoughts than meets the eye; thoughts are the driving engines behind our actions. A thought can be the source of creation or destruction in the world!" Butterfly tried to help his friend make sense of it.

"Thoughts, driving engines, creation, and destruction of worlds? My head is spinning with it!" it was too much for Cockerel's young mind. His plumage was ruffled up, an outside reflection of the confusion in his mind.

Wind, on the other hand, had trouble coming to terms with Cockerel's sudden changes in appearance, especially when no breeze was involved.

"A thought can turn into action and reaction, just like a seedling turns into a big tree, or like a baby grows into an adult!" Butterfly adopted another line of argument.

"I never thought of it that way!" he confessed, finally grasping the idea.

Butterfly smiled inside: he found Cockerel's naivety very endearing, indeed!

"The power of our thoughts makes the world go around and sits at the root of everything, good and bad! That's why it's so important to be watchful of your thoughts and words; they can build others up, as well as bring them down. When you release your thoughts in words, you give them life and put things in motion!"

"It sounds very complicated and scary!" Cockerel voiced out his honest opinion.

"It sounds more complicated than it really is; you only need one person determined enough to turn thought into action, and you've got an idea coming to life!"

Butterfly's words made quite an impression on Cockerel who fell quiet pondering over them. His eyes rested on two fluffy dandelion seedlings floating on the wings of a light gust of wind.

"The scary part of it all is when sadness and anger get hold of you, and your thoughts become harsh words before you know it. This is when we have to be on guard the most, take responsibility for our words and actions before they cause havoc and destruction beyond repair, like as many deadly bolts of lightning!"

Cockerel put on a serious face, and frowned anxiously.

"No need to worry too much about it now, you've got your entire life in front of you and time is on your side! It will naturally come to you when you are ready for it! Going back to our story, I think I owe Rica an answer to his question, don't I?" he turned his attention to the duckling again.

"You haven't forgotten about it!" Rica was very impressed with Butterfly's ability to hold onto a thought and come back to it after a while. "You were telling Cockerel how you managed to get hold of me the second time around!" he reminded his friend.

"Spot on, young drake!" Butterfly praised Rica. "Upon my return from your house, I followed the footpath to the lake assuming that you would head to the water to have a swim and de-stress, like any duckling would do under the circumstances. Luckily, there's something for everybody in nature..."

"You are wandering off again from our story!" Rica pointed out smiling.

"When you are right, you are right, young drake!" Butterfly replied, happy to see Rica full of purpose and focused on the task. "I was telling you that I flew to the lake where I couldn't find you, but I witnessed the baby swallow falling in the water and, despite our efforts, couldn't do a thing to help him. At that point, finding you became even more important, as it was obvious you were the only one able to swim out and save the baby swallow."

Rica felt awkwardly proud to hear that he had been the first creature Butterfly thought of summoning up throughout such a dramatic and serious incident. He sat still, unable to react in any way, but for Wind who sneaked behind him and gave him a gentle nudge over the head, which looked more like a nod to the others. Butterfly took it on board as a sign of approval and happily continued the story:

"Eventually, we found you in Cockerel's company," Butterfly unexpectedly reached the end of his story.

"That shows that our encounter was totally random!" Cockerel concluded.

"Our encounter? Definitely random!" Rica agreed.

Suddenly realizing the full meaning of his words, Rica swallowed hard and stared hard at Butterfly.

"What's up, duck?" the latter took up on it.

"It just dawned on me that I was the only one who left home in search for a friend. You and Cockerel didn't care much about that! That makes me the only one here in desperate need of a friend! Yes, the only one!" Rica kept repeating the words getting gloomier by the second.

"What's the problem?" Butterfly couldn't cope with Rica's quick change in moods.

"You said yourself that in the morning you went to look about your favorite flower bud and just happened to run into me afterwards..."

"I still don't get what the problem is!" Butterfly couldn't see any fault with what he did.

"You've got your flower bud to make you happy, you don't need a friend like me!" Rica felt very sorry for himself.

"Now, there, there... Enough with the crazy talk! I went to see about the flower bud because I have a duty to care for all plants in nature and because I love it! What's one got to do with the other? Why would that stop me from making other friends?"

Wind blew in front of him this way and that way, living proof of Butterfly's words.

"Yes, for instance, Wind and Cockerel and you, duckling! Anyone would be proud to have all of you as friends." Butterfly argued.

"Actually, I was in search for a friend myself," Cockerel reasserted his intention. "I wasn't necessarily looking for you, of course! How could I? This morning when I set out on my way, I had no idea you existed. But fate brought us together and I couldn't be happier about that. Why are you so bothered about it?"

"Cockerel is right; even if our encounter had been completely accidental, we have been through an amazing adventure together, and that's no small thing! What are your thoughts about it all?" Butterfly turned to them. "And think of this: there is more to come with the swallows spreading the word about us far and wide; fame is awaiting and who knows what more!" Butterfly concluded.

They all peeked at one another and each admitted to himself that Butterfly's argument was flawless. In the end, Cockerel decided to venture another topic and change the atmosphere:

"What about your parents, brothers and sisters, Butterfly? Where are they?"

Butterfly's eyes went wide as he was caught unaware.

"It depends which part of my life you are referring to!" Butterfly answered puzzled.

It was the others' turn to exchange baffled glances.

"What do you mean by that?"

"You must remember that butterflies are born twice in this life! We are the only species who enjoy the privilege! In fact, our life cycle confirms the much-disputed theory of reincarnation. If you want, you can think of us as a more rudimentary type of angels: we are born, develop for a while, die only to be reborn again; the story of life and afterlife in a nutshell! That also explains why butterfly can't mix with anything evil in the world!"

"My goodness, that's a thought for you today, as if it hadn't been eventful enough so far!" Cockerel exclaimed looking Rica in the eye. The duckling felt a frog in his throat and chose to remain quiet.

"Are all your family well and alive?"

Butterfly had been taking them down a path which was too hard to comprehend for his friends. But who could blame them? They were still very young and inexperienced, and the things Butterfly was talking about were completely new to them. He shook his head gently to get rid of negative thoughts and decided it was time for an uplift in the mood. Thus, with assistance of his good friend, he took to the wings and performed a quick-paced dance up in the air, very much to the entertainment of Rica and Cockerel.

"Look, guys, you might not be the most knowledgeable as far as butterflies are concerned, but you are great fun to be around and I love being friends with you, even though I never intended to in the first place!" Butterfly told them candidly, without realizing how brutally honest his words were.

"Why didn't you intend making friends with us from the very beginning?" Cockerel and Rica asked in unison, "You seemed happy enough to get the conversation started and to play games with us!"

"I haven't got much time for casual friendships!" Butterfly admitted.

"If you have no time for making friends, what do you have time for? What can be more rewarding than genuine friendship?" Cockerel appeared rather intrigued.

"My dear friends, my life span is very short compared to other creatures." Butterfly accepted to satisfy their curiosity.

"And why is that?" they carried on asking.

"Considering that we are born twice within the same life cycle, it can't be any other way: in exchange for that privilege, we live a short and somewhat lonely life."

"Are you saying that you are alone in the world? An orphan, maybe?" Rica and Cockerel were in a state of shock.

"I'm not lonely in that way; the entire nature is my family!" Butterfly replied.

"Don't you have a mother; a father and siblings like us?" Rica murmured.

"I've just told you that, unlike any other creature on Earth, butterflies are born twice within the same life cycle."

"What does that mean?" Cockerel found himself at a loss.

"I am born of a mother and a father when I first come into the world, but once my second birth happens, I have to leave them all behind and take to the wings!" he made it clear for them.

"Why leave them all behind? You said that you are born twice within the same life cycle," Cockerel insisted.

"It is as you say, indeed, but with my second birth I gain access to a different dimension and I come to life as somebody completely changed from who I used to be!" Butterfly tried to give him an insight into things.

"It's all Greek to me, my friend," Cockerel confessed his inability to make sense of things. "Can you break it down to smaller bites for me, please?"

"Our souls become purer and more elevated with every single life we are born into, until we finally join the great Universal Spirit... My life span is very short, but that doesn't bother me at all, as I see myself as part and parcel of nature which is infinite; think, for example, of a falling star travelling through the sky: the death of the star is not its end, but a new beginning as stardust somewhere else in the universe. In the same way, butterflies look forward to the promise of a new adventure with every life we take up on. Besides, we have a duty of care towards other creatures; we bring joy and happiness to all beings in nature, big and small. It is our way of gaining access to immortality. In other words, you are the key to eternal life for me!" Butterfly concluded triumphantly only to realize the shock on his friends face hadn't diminished a bit.

"We are the key to eternal life for you?" Cockerel and Rica could only echo Butterfly's words, while scraping to grasp some meaning.

"That's always the way," Butterfly confirmed, "you know what they say: once seen, never forgotten, and that's the highway to eternal life for us!!"

"Highway to eternal life?" Rica muttered. "No offence, Butterfly, but have you been sniffing magic mushrooms this morning?"

"I did something much better than that: I've made good friends with you, and I'm sure that the two of you will fondly remember me in future, and this is my way of cheating death: we live on through the memories of those who remember us for as long as they can. Even when I'm no longer part of this world, I'll still be..."

"Where will you be?" Rica and Cockerel held their breath in anticipation.

"I'll be in your hearts and minds and you'll be able to summon me every time you need a friend at your side!"

"How is that possible?" Cockerel felt he needed more facts to be able to believe it.

"I'll appear in your dreams, and I'll always be part of your psyche in this life and in the next ones! But beware, as great privilege comes with great responsibility!" Butterfly warned his friends.

"What kind of responsibility?"

"We are responsible for the influence we have on those around us and for the good, or the bad, that we choose to leave behind... Butterflies have a special mission to carry out in this life: we are the keepers of goodwill in the world and the fine task of restoring the balance of the universe in that respect is all ours! With all those things to do within such a short life, you can easily imagine that we don't get much time to ourselves..."

Discontent again for being forgotten about by everybody, Wind had been spinning his tail for a while and was on the verge of raising a twister. Luckily, Butterfly noticed the danger and addressed him appeasingly:

"It doesn't mean that your role is less important in the world, my friend! Quite the opposite, I can't imagine what we'd do without you!"

Easily pleased by his friends' reconciliatory words, Wind squashed the little storm as quickly as he had brought it up. With that problem solved, Butterfly could pick up the chat where he had left it.

"Here is what I suggest: why don't we all agree to be friends forever and ever, and I'll be happy to share the joy of looking after the flowerbud with you!" Butterfly generously proposed.

"That's a great idea!" Rica and Cockerel accepted the invitation straight away.

Cockerel puffed up his chest in excitement. "We've only known each other for a few hours, and we already have a history of adventure together. If that's not the sign of a life-long friendship, I don't know what is!" Cockerel trumpeted cheerfully.

"Being so young in the world meant that Rica and Cockerel couldn't have known much about many things, including the very interesting life cycle of butterflies," commented Mom. "Butterflies hatch from eggs into caterpillars, and from the very first day of life they have to find their way into the world, with the nature around them as the only mother and father they know, the only guiding force which teaches them the survival skills they need... Butterfly, however, could not bring himself to tell his new friends the bare truth for fear that the many differences between them might have put them off. Wisdom comes with age, some say, but despite Butterfly's young age in his current life, he held enough wisdom to accurately assess a situation: too much information for such young minds could have caused more harm than good, and in some cases, it could have brought about unwanted negative emotions, such as jealousy and envy... We sometimes fall victims to the illusion that butterflies live in big swarms and they are blessed with large families: they can come together to perform magical dance routines, they can flock in on lawns full of blossoming flowers, but few of us realize they are actually solitary creatures.

"When butterflies emerge from their cocoons, they will have already earned through suffering their right to holiness. As caterpillars, they are but humble crawlers, looked down upon and despised by everybody, ruthlessly hunted down by predators. But the ordeal they have to endure earns them the rightful place amongst the angels of heaven, for they are just that: the earthly embodiment of holy creatures. In their new form, they can understand suffering better than anyone else after having experienced it themselves... They are a sign of divine mercy and a role-model for us all, but we are too busy living in our little bubbles and too blind to the world around us..." Mom explained.

"Wind, however, a grandchild of Ancient Wind, had been following Butterfly around taking everything in, as his granddad had advised him back in the days of his early childhood..."

"Mom, why didn't Butterfly reveal more about himself to his new friends?" I asked, taking advantage of the short break in the story-telling.

"I can only guess why, my dear boy: perhaps he thought the difference between them would drive Rica and Cockerel away; or maybe he realized they were not ready to deal with that sort of information yet; last, but not least, he could have done so out of humility... You must know that all wise creatures are also humble..."

"What exactly is humility, Mom?" I continued with my questions.

"Well, well, I might soon have to do what Butterfly did if you keep shooting out one question after another!" Mom teased me with a smile. "Humility, my little ones, is the mother of love and care for all beings on earth..."

But Mom was right: I felt like Cockerel in her story asking all those questions. The more questions Mom answered, the less I understood of it all!

"Did they become friends for life after all?" I changed the topic.

"They did, and they are friends even to this day!" Mom let us know with laughter in her eyes.

"Over-excited at the prospect of having such fine friends for life, Cockerel charged to hug Rica and Butterfly. Surprised at the unexpected manifestation of affection, Rica ducked out of the way.

"What are you on about?" he demanded an explanation for Cockerel's impetuous behavior.

"Don't you think this is great! The two of us and Butterfly, friends for life?" Cockerel cried out excitedly.

But that didn't go down very well with Wind: where was his place in this circle of friendship?

"Count Wind in, as well!" Butterfly intervened to correct the situation.

"Brilliant! I think all of you make awesome friends!"

"Why did you duck out of the way, then?" Cockerel asked surprised.

"I can't help thinking of what my late grandma once told me while spinning yarns in front of the fire and watching shooting stars race across the summer's night sky: she said that best friends don't hold secrets from each other!"

"But that shouldn't be a problem, should it? We've only met one another, and I wouldn't have thought we have anything to hide. I, for one, have no secrets at all!" Butterfly declared and opened his wings wide to display his true colors in plain sight. Wind followed suit and rushed through letting everybody see how transparent he was.

"It's nothing that comes to mind which I would keep from you guys," Cockerel joined in.

"By the looks of it, I'm the only one who's got a secret!" Rica confessed lowering his eyes.

"In this case, you better spill the beans and free yourself of such a burden, duckling! I mean it, spit it out and you'll feel happier for it!" Cockerel urged his friend.

"I lied to you about what happened when I found you unconscious under the bush!" Rica admitted a bit ashamed.

"You lied to me? Why did you do that?" Cockerel found it difficult to comprehend.

Rica peeked towards Butterfly to see his reaction, but the latter shrugged his shoulders unwilling to judge anyone before he had heard the whole story.

"Why did you lie to him?" he eventually asked in a neutral voice.

"It wasn't the seeds falling from the sky that knocked you out!"

"What seeds are you talking about?" Butterfly quipped, dying to find out more about it. Rica put his hand in the pocket and took out a handful of seeds.

"These seeds I'm talking about! Perhaps I should say: these seeds are not what I should be talking about!"

The sunlight glowing on the seeds made them look like little strands of gold.

"Are you going to tell me what really happened!?" Cockerel pleaded for the truth.

"Here is what really happened: a little worm dropped from the beak of a cuckoo flying by and knocked you out!"

Cockerel expected anything but that! He stared at his friend wondering whether that one was pulling his leg again. Rica continued:

"When you fainted, you trapped the little worm under your right wing," Rica described the picture he had come across when he first discovered Cockerel.

"I thought your story about seeds falling from the sky didn't hold water…" he scolded Rica.

"I had to think on my feet and come up with something believable; now I can tell you that I had those seeds in my pocket from home in case I became peckish on the way…"

"I still can't see why you lied to me?" Cockerel tried to shed some light on the matter.

"I was afraid that you might want to take revenge on the little worm who was very much a victim like you!" Rica finally revealed his motif.

"How did you work that one out?" Cockerel kept on questioning him

"The little worm told me what happened!" Rica answered.

"So, you had time for a full conversation, did you?"

"We did!"

"Where is he?"

"Who's he?" Cockerel's fast questioning threw Rica off the track.

"I'm talking about the little worm, who else?" Cockerel felt his comb and grimaced with pain.

"How would I know where he is?" it was Rica's turn to counteract. "Wait a bit, why are you so interested in his whereabouts!" Rica panicked.

"What kind of question is that? I'd like to make friends with him, of course! I was in search for a friend and he dropped right on me from the sky… literally! That's fate at work and answered prayers call for a celebration! When you think about it, today I saved another life, apart from that of the baby swallow! We may as well extend our circle of friends to include a little worm, isn't it?"

Then, without any warning, he started body-searching Rica who burst into laughter since he was very ticklish.

"What are you trying to do to me, is this some sort of devilish punishment for having lied to you?" Rica could hardly string the words together in between fits of laughter.

"I'm just looking for the little worm!"

"He's back there, well hidden in the bush where I found you!" Rica eventually managed to pull out of his friend's hands and compose himself.

"What are we waiting for? Let's all go back find him!" Cockerel called out. "Do you remember the way back?"

"I do…"

"Are we all ready for take-off?" Cockerel checked on the others.

"What's the rush?" Rica tried to calm him down.

"We've got to go now, otherwise we'll never find him! He's probably departing the place as we speak, or he may well be far on his way to a destination only he knows!" Cockerel paced up and down.

"I wouldn't worry about that! He took shelter in the next bush and was in no hurry to get anywhere!" Rica reassured his friend.

"I know how you feel, because I feel the same way towards my flowerbud!" Butterfly intervened.

"You are right, that's exactly how I feel!" Rica replied, and his right wing instinctively touched his chest.

"How did that come about?" Cockerel and Butterfly wanted to know.

"Earlier in the day I stopped and had a little chat with a cuckoo who was looking for a little worm with a star on his forehead. At first, I thought it was you as a caterpillar," Rica turned to Butterfly, "and I decided to send him in the wrong direction and rid you of him!"

"That's right, you did that!" Butterfly agreed.

"How do you know about it?" Rica exclaimed.

"I was secretly watching you from a distance!"

"Secretly? So, you have your little secrets, as well!" Rica told him off.

"Come on, duckling, knock it off!" Butterfly joked

"Have you forgiven me yet?" Rica asked hopeful.

"Forgive you for what, brother?" Butterfly squinted at him.

"For being so narky, and so suspicious and for taking your joke the wrong way..." Rica mumbled under his breath.

"Are you serious? I've already forgotten about all those silly things!"

"Are we friends, then?"

"But of course we are, I thought you've worked that one out by now!" Butterfly stifled a giggle and stepped forward to share a man-hug with Rica and Cockerel, while Wind was running circles around them sealing their bond.

"Shall we go now?" Cockerel pulled out of the hug first, acting on impulse as usual.

"Where are we going?" the others took a moment to get on the same wavelength.

"Let's make our way back to the bush where the worm took shelter!"

"Let's!" the others agreed.

They traced back their steps until they reached the bush, but as soon as they got there, a funny noise caught their attention. Rica smiled mysteriously.

"Why are you smiling?" Cockerel whispered to him.

"I have an inkling that the little worm we are looking for is somewhere nearby!" Rica announced him in a low voice.

"You reckon?" Cockerel was unsure.

Light-footed as he was, Wind rushed ahead of the others only to discover a mole lying belly-up on a strangely shaped object which looked like a smooth, oval, silver-colored stone picked up on the white beaches of a remote tropical island. By the looks of it, Mole had just finished his lunch and was resting, licking his fingers and chewing on the flavors still lingering on his tongue.

Under the new and unexpected circumstances, Rica refrained from putting forward his theory about the crackling noises, waiting to see the new situation unfold. A quick exchange of silent glances enabled the four friends to agree on the plan of action. But as they were getting ready for retreat, Mole suddenly stopped from his afternoon routine and sniffed the air around. At a glance, Cockerel realized Rica had stepped in bird droppings which stirred up the smell alerting Mole about their presence. Without thinking twice about it, Wind swished through a bunch of fragrant flowers and blew the scent towards the spot where Mole was lazing about, trying to cover up the stench rising from Rica's soiled feet. But it was too little, too late. Mole had already stood up and, facing them, wet a finger in his own saliva and put it above his head to check the direction of the wind.

"Well, well, what have we here?"

He then started talking in a squeaky voice as if addressing someone nearby.

"When were you going to let me know that we've got company?" he asked, hardly controlling the curiosity which came through in his voice.

The four friends had a good look around, but couldn't see anyone else. Slowly, they made the first steps backwards, but Rica accidentally snapped a dry stick under his foot, which gave them away for good. In a flash, Mole picked up a beautifully decorated stick from up his sleeve and skilfully aimed it in Rica's direction before he threw it.

While the hollow stick was turning and tossing in the air, they heard a gentle sound coming from inside it. Wind, the most curious of them all, rushed to check it out and meandered his way through it: it was a tiny recorder, intricately crafted and looking more like a little piece of jewelry than a musical instrument.

At that moment, something extraordinary happened; a small voice which seemed to materialize out of thin air replied to Mole:

"It's a couple of chicks!"

"A couple of chicks, you say?" Mole repeated.

"Yes, a couple of bird chicks!"

"Bird chicks!" Mole echoed again the small voice.

"I've asked a question and I haven't gotten an answer yet!" Mole got in a strop, but tried to calm down his temper by producing a toothpick which he started using deftly.

"I was telling you that it's a duckling and a baby-cockerel straight ahead of you!" the voice informed him, intentionally avoiding mentioning anything about Butterfly.

"I'm in no mood for jokes, you know…" Mole retorted gravely, as he fished out of his teeth some rotting flesh, sniffed it for a few moments before he put it back in his mouth and gave it a good chew. The four friends stared at one another, their stomachs churning.

"Are you telling me the truth?" Mole asked out of the blue.

Although he couldn't see anything, he sensed there was somebody else apart from the bird chicks.

"What kind of question is that?" the small voice spoke back.

"I can smell vulture droppings, you know!" Mole said menacingly.

Rica froze in his position, only his eyes stared around; there were no vultures in sight, but it had become clear by now that Mole used somebody else to 'see' his way around.

"I swear I'm telling you the truth," the small trembling voice pleaded. "Why do you even bother asking me if you don't believe a word I say?"

Driven by curiosity, Butterfly looped around in the air and positioned himself behind Mole, where he finally discovered where the small voice was coming from: a tiny dun-bug with teary eyes was resting on a pile of bird waste. Mole controlled him by a leash made of spider thread which deftly connected a solid ring made of Valerian root placed around his finger with a spiky collar firmly tightened around the dun-bug's neck.

"Why did Mole keep the dun-bug captive on a leash?" I asked, impatient for an explanation.

"Mole used the dun-bug as his eyes, which allowed him to move around freely and keep out of danger. If you pay attention to the rest of the story, you'll work out yourself why!" Mom told me.

"Mom, I'm all ears when you tell us stories, and sometimes I can't wait to find out what's next!" I complained.

"As you all know, moles are not able to see in daylight. As long as they are underground, they are safe and comfortable, but once they come to the surface, they become weak and vulnerable. Thus, Mole hatched a cunning plan to enslave the dun-bug and use him as his eyes on the ground; that way, he could catch his food and roam around freely, against the odds!"

"Why are the odds against moles roaming freely on the surface of the earth?" I couldn't help asking another question.

"Because God sentenced them to living their lives in the darkness of the underground!"

"Why would God do something like that?"

"Because once a mole decided to take a terrible revenge on his enemies, and that made them all fall from God's grace!"

"But what made that mole want so badly to take revenge on his enemies?"

"That is a whole new story, and I'll have to tell it to you some other time!" Mom replied.

"Shall we continue this story now, Mom?" I implored her.

"I thought you'd never ask!" she ruffled my hair with a smile.

"No more questions, I promise! Not for the time being, anyway!"

Mom nodded in agreement and carried on:

"After solving the mystery of the small voice, Butterfly returned to his friends and beaconed to them quietly to check out the ground for Dun-Bug. Mole kept sniffing the air; the draught created by Butterfly's wings had brought to him a familiar, yet hard to identify scent...

Rica and Cockerel peeked in the direction indicated by Butterfly and noticed Dun-Bug, who waved at them. You could tell by the look in his eyes he was not happy at all.

"Listen to me, you little scumbag, you better not play smart with me!" Mole raised his voice, and the four friends could tell by the rudeness in his voice that he was addressing Dun-Bug.

Mole yanked the leash and poor Dun-Bug nearly died by strangulation.

"My Goodness, it didn't even cross my mind, I swear on my eyes!" Dun-Bug pleaded again in a sorry voice.

"Stop bumping your gums stupidly, scumbag! I warned you before that you shouldn't swear on your eyes, they are not yours to give them up any way you want, they belong to me now!" Mole admonished him.

"Yes, master, I won't swear on my eyes again!"

"Why aren't these spring-chicks saying hello to me? Or, are they trying to pull a fast one?" Mole let on his spite which he had managed to hold back until then

Fully aware as to why Mole was so brutal to Dun-Bug, Rica intervened:

"Hello there, Mole!"

His ego finally satisfied by this sign of respect, Mole weakened his hold on the leash and replied:

"Hello back, you little yellow ball of fluff!"

"How do you know I'm a yellow fluff-ball?" Rica was in a state of shock since Dun-Bug never mentioned anything about the color of his plumage, and Mole couldn't see a thing!

"You sound like one!" Mole retorted in a croaky voice. "What's bringing you here, so far away from home?"

"What about you? What's bringing you here?" Cockerel interfered trying to distract him while going around the place looking for the little worm.

"Who do we have here? A little red fluff-ball, and a cheeky one for that matter!" Mole commented quickly turning his head to face Cockerel.

It was Cockerel's turn to experience an eerie feeling at Mole's accurate assumptions about him. Mole must have been around for a while and he must have come across quite a few ducklings and cockerels in his life, most likely by exploiting another poor helpless creature to 'see' them.

"I'm a baby cockerel!" he answered quickly as he kept moving around to befuddle sly Mole.

"I've worked that out all right!" Mole said.

"When did you work it out?" Cockerel kept him busy.

"As soon as you opened your beak!" Mole informed him, then he began muttering to himself:

"You filthy fowl! Unexpected encounters are the last thing on my agenda, especially at lunchtime!"

Wind, who was circling around the place, was close enough to hear him: there was more to Mole than met the eye, and they better be aware of it!

At the end of this nasty outpour of words, Mole cleared his throat and, acting as affable as he could, he addressed Cockerel:

"You'll be glad to find out that I'm very fond of your kind: I don't know what I would do without a cockerel's morning cry which wakes me up every day!"

While Cockerel was keeping Mole busy talking, Butterfly joined in the search for the little worm. Wind was diligently pushing branches out of the way, while the others scrutinized the ground. But they didn't find anything apart from dead leaves and berries. You would have thought that a big broom had been going around sweeping off everything else before their arrival. Cockerel looked at Wind who shrugged his shoulders:

"Perhaps the arrival of Mole made everybody run away!"

Wind shrugged again and nodded at the same time: that was a strong possibility! Cockerel's eyes widened all of a sudden and the others could tell something was going on in his mind, something which crossed their minds nearly straight away: what if the little worm had been eaten up by Mole?

In the meantime, Mole, oblivious to their suspicions, continued to talk to Cockerel:

"This is my home, I live here!"

"You do?" Rica's voice gave away his doubt.

Yanking the leash again, Mole urged Dun-Bug to confirm his version of the story. The latter nodded diligently in the direction of the new arrivals.

"I do, indeed!" he emphasized with a sneer.

Rica squinted trying to see where exactly Mole's home was. He felt bad about leaving behind the little worm whose chances of survival seemed slimmer and slimmer with Mole foraging around for food. Had he known about it, he could have *done something at the time. But when he stretched his neck looking for Mole's home, there was no hole in the ground.*

After a few moments of intent search, Rica's eyes met Dun-Bug's, the latter picked a seedling out of his pocket and threw it in the direction of an oak leaf lying on the ground at some distance. Mole picked up on the noise immediately and became alert, but Wind ruffled a few dead leaves confusing her again.

Rica assumed that Dun-Bug was throwing seedlings around at whim, so he didn't pay much attention to him. Butterfly, however, understood it was more than that, so he flew over to Rica and whispered something in his ear

"Ideal place for a home!" Rica spoke out addressing Mole.

"I should say so! Welcome to my humble home!" Mole said half-jokingly, half menacingly.

"Humble it may be, but very well placed for food foraging!" Rica replied.

"We hope you don't mind uninvited guests!"

"Whatever! I'm not fussy!" Mole agreed.

"Have you had something nice for lunch?"

"Yes, I have, thank you for asking!"

"Glad to hear it! What was it, if you don't mind me asking?" Rica tried to catch Mole unaware.

"Why do you want to know?" Mole avoided direct answers.

"I wasn't going to tell you this, but the noise of your slurping, gulping and swigging led us to you, and got us in a right mood to have a taste of the same thing that you were eating with so much gusto! Besides, we think meeting you here today is a prime opportunity to get to know you better; after all, you are such a mysterious creature and we would like to find out more about you: what you eat, what kind of lifestyle you've got, what does your home look like on the inside…" Rica went on until Mole interrupted:

"You want to see the inside of my home?" he burst out choking. "Have you been saying that you followed the noise of my slurping, gulping and swigging to get here?" Mole couldn't believe his ears. He had been very slack in the way he behaved; luckily, it had only been a couple of chicks who picked up on the noise, and not a sly fox which would have been glad to have stuffed mole for lunch!

"That's right: hearing you eating lunch made us change direction and come this way!" Rica emphasized noticing his words made an impression on Mole.

Cockerel was following the whole conversation from under the bush, waiting to see where his friends' plan would lead them.

Mole felt confused. Ever since these uninvited guests broke the peace and quiet of his sanctuary, Mole could distinguish a muffled and rhythmic beat which he couldn't explain. It was driving him mad.

"If you must know, I had a worm for lunch, a little measly worm which wasn't doing anyone any good. I did a favor to Mother-Nature by putting an end to the little pest's life. Parasites like that shouldn't be allowed to live, and by doing that I declare myself Doctor Mole who saves the world from worms!" Mole commented pompously.

Butterfly shuddered listening to Mole but avoided intervening in any way since he had heard of the Legend of the Mole and the historic enmity between moles and worms.

Mole yawned a long yawn, pleased with himself.

"Nicely done, Doctor Mole!" Rica said ironically, while the others were still recovering from the shock.

"Thank you, my dear boy! To be quite honest, the little pest was just an appetizer, I could quite easily eat a few hundreds of his kind!" Mole confessed, unable to read Rica's sardonic tone.

Rica and Butterfly tiptoed to Dun-Bug and whispered something in his ear. Dun-Bug raised his eyes to the sky and put his hands together over his chest in a gesture of gratitude for something he had been praying for a long time.

Gathering it was time for some action, Butterfly nodded to Rica and Cockerel: they were going to take care of Mole. Butterfly glided to the side of the bush where he could see the end of a silver thread showing from underneath some leaves. He pulled and tugged at it and out came a little leaf coated in a fine spider web. It was a thing of rare beauty! Butterfly started to unravel the fine thread while making sure that the dewdrops kept on the leaf for the benefit of the plant which swayed to and fro gracefully. Butterfly bowed gallantly before returning to Dun-Bug. Rica and Cockerel watched him from a distance but stayed put on their own task. Everybody had to do their bit if the plan was to be successful.

"Just to be clear, Mole, are we talking here about a little worm with a star on its forehead?" Rica pushed the envelope.

Mole felt his mouth watering at the thought, and was only able to answer after swallowing it.

"Are you talking about the famous species of the bamboo worm?" Mole asked back licking his lips.

Rica and Cockerel stared at each other: they didn't have a clue what Mole was talking about. Cockerel shrugged, while Rica focused on keeping Mole distracted:

"Yes, it's the bamboo worm that has a star for a horn!" Rica quipped seemingly cheerful although his heart was heavy imagining the grim ending of the poor little worm.

Rica's apparent light-heartedness did not fool Wind, however, who closed in swiftly from the side and captured a sorrowful sigh which the duckling involuntarily let out. In order to cheer him up a bit, Wind had a mischievous thought; he modelled Rica's steamy breath to resemble the bird droppings which he had stepped into earlier, and drew nearer Mole, winking at his friends. With a dexterous move of his tail, Wind tickled Mole's eardrum to trigger a yawn, and when Mole opened his mouth wide to release it, Wind took the opportunity and placed the steamy figurine in it. Rica and Cockerel nearly burst out in to laughter but managed to control themselves at the last moment. Wind was disapprovingly squinting at them, although he had cooked out the idea in the first place. Mole, however, was blissfully unaware of the fun the children were poking at him, and carried on chatting with Rica.

"I wish it had been a bamboo worm, but unfortunately no, it was just an ordinary wriggler!" Mole admitted.

"Why, what's so special about the bamboo worm?" Rica continued his questions with a smile of relief on his face.

"The bamboo worm is very rare to come across in this part of the world because bamboo doesn't grow here. You'd be lucky to get to see one, let alone eat it!" Mole informed him proud of his vast knowledge.

"Why is it such a big thing getting to see one of them?" Rica went on, keeping a close eye on Butterfly who was carrying out their secret plan.

"The bamboo worm plays an important role in the cuckoo's life-cycle, as they help these birds assert their identity! Can you imagine that?" Mole put on a very knowledgeable face.

In the meantime, Butterfly's plan was well on its way to success. Dun-Bug had been set free from his leash and was getting ready to take off when he was warned by Butterfly to keep still and quiet and not alert Mole. Butterfly had one more thing to do: he tied the free end of the leash to a poppy-flower head lying nearby. At that moment, Mole picked up a floral scent travelling in the air and became alert

"I can smell somebody else around here, Dun-Bug! Who is it? You are not hiding anything from me, are you?" Mole asked.

Fortunately for Dun-Bug, his time in Mole's service had just come to an end and Butterfly grabbed him by the horns and flew away with him. Faced with an unusual silence, Mole pricked his ears in the air trying to get to grips with the new situation.

"I'm talking to you, little scumbag!" Mole raised his voice. "Have you gone deaf, or died altogether at the sight of all these birds who could gulp you in a jiffy?" Mole roared with a brief laughter.

Mole pulled harshly at the leash, and when the far end reached him, touched it to check on the prisoner, but all he could feel was a dry prickly poppy flower-head. Mole squished the dry flower head in anger as he realized that his victim had escaped.

"You little scavenger, come back here! We've had an agreement! Get yourself back here at once!" Mole started to sound desperate more than threatening. It suddenly dawned on him that the new arrivals had plotted all along to liberate his prisoner.

"I should have known from the very beginning that you are but a couple of ungrateful, good-for-nothing chicks, but I welcomed you in my home against my best instinct! You better give me back that filthy Dun-Bug right now. He is mine and I have the right of life and death over him!"

Thinking on his feet, Rica improvised.

"Run, everybody run as fast as you can!" he yelled at the top of his lungs.

"What now? What's going on?!" Mole panicked.

"A great big vulture is coming straight for us, faster than a bolt of lightning!" Rica played it out.

"What are you saying? A vulture?" Mole flipped over on his feet with a sudden move which caused his old joints to creak painfully.

"Run for your lives, the vulture is coming down on us fast!" Rica urged.

Hardly had Rica finished his warning that Mole nimbly jumped from the stone and landed squarely in the center of the oak leaf and disappeared through it as if the earth had opened up and swallowed him whole! The oak leaf was a skilfully designed camouflage for the entrance to Mole's home. Split through the middle just enough to let Mole in and out easily, once used it came back to its natural shape, cleverly concealing the entrance to Mole's burrow.

Taken aback by Rica's shouts, Cockerel really thought they were in an emergency situation and quickly sheltered himself underneath a leafy branch from which the little worm with a star on its forehead had witnessed the whole scene. But Cockerel was too busy looking after himself to notice the little creature next to him. Soon after, Rica joined Cockerel underneath the leafy branch.

"Where have you gone?" Rica called out to his friend, but Cockerel was too scared to answer. His eyes still adjusting to the dim light in the foliage, Rica banged his head badly, but stifled a cry of pain for fear that it might draw Mole back. The duckling closed his eyes and waited until the sharp pain subsided a bit. When he finally opened his eyes again he had the worm with a star on his forehead looking straight at him! While rubbing his painful bump, Rica's mouth fell open: that was a nice surprise! From where he took refuge, Cockerel could only see Rica staring at a branch at his eye-level and touching his sore head.

"Hey, duckling, you better hide quickly here with me! If the vulture saw us, he'll keep searching until he finds us!

But Rica was so overwhelmed by the sudden appearance of Little Worm, that he paid attention to nothing else but that! An awkward smile blossomed on his beak, leaving Cockerel totally baffled at the sight! Why was the duckling staring at a fixed spot and smiling? Could that blow at the head be so bad? Cockerel mustered all his courage and stepped out of his hiding place, only to see the object of his friend's attention. But Little Worm withdrew quickly, not knowing what to make of Cockerel. Rica opened his mouth to speak, but Cockerel nodded at him and the duckling stepped back. Cockerel addressed Little Worm in a whispering tone:

"Hello there, Little Worm, you've got nothing to fear from me! We've come back with the best of intentions, believe me!"

"It's the truth!" Rica confirmed.

"I know you are telling the truth, but I have my doubts about him!" Little Worm confessed to Rica.

"You shouldn't doubt me at all! I'm as truthful as he is!" Cockerel fought his corner striving to win over Little Worm's trust at the same time.

"Are you, really?" Little Worm asked for reassurance again.

Nodding his head, Cockerel edged forward, and after having had a good peep at Worm, he burst out enthusiastically in Rica's direction:

"When you first told me, I thought you made it up, but I see that Little Worm really has a star on his forehead!"

Little Worm checked them out with a scrutinizing look, and eventually asked:

"Are you two friends?"

"We are!" Rica and Cockerel agreed in unison.

"Since when?" it was Little Worm's turn to be surprised; only a few hours earlier the two chicks were strangers to each other. Not quite sure whether it was good news for him, Little Worm wriggled backwards preparing for retreat.

"Don't go anywhere, please!" Rica pleaded. "We've made friends today!"

"Yes, we've made friends after he rescued you!" Cockerel explained.

"After he rescued me?" Little Worm tried to place the events in chronological order and make sense of them.

"And after he rescued me, as well! It was all meant to happen so that we could meet and become friends! In fact, this is the reason we came back for: to find you!" Cockerel chirped happily.

"It was meant to happen?" Little Worm struggled to keep up with his rationale.

"Yes, God planned it in such a way that you fell on my head and knocked me out, only for this duckling to show up, rescue you, rescue me and all three of us end up being good friends!" Cockerel summed it up for Little Worm.

"I see you've told him everything about our encounter!" Little Worm turned to Rica.

"Yes, good friends always tell the truth to each other," Rica admitted.

"And I see you've been very gracious about it all!" Little Worm turned to Cockerel this time.

"I consider myself lucky enough to have been shared with you two a moment of grace!" Cockerel gave him an insight into his thinking.

A strange silence took over and the three of them smiled awkwardly at one another. The rustle of disturbed leaves alerted them to someone coming; Butterfly and Dun-Bug landed next to their friends.

"What are you doing hiding here?" Butterfly couldn't understand. "Mole had cleared off a while ago... unless... a vulture is really circling around the place!" he whispered cautiously peeping from under the bush.

But instead of a ruthless vulture, Butterfly noticed a leaf shivering and a tiny face peeking from behind. Wind went closer and blew up the leaf which revealed to everybody Worm hiding there. But Little Worm had had time to grow comfortable with his new acquaintances by now and the arrival of the new comers didn't seem to bother him a bit.

"This is the one and only Little Worm for whom we came back!" Rica introduced his wiggly friend to the others.

Butterfly took off and landed shortly after on the twig in front of Little Worm:

"Hi there, I hope you don't mind me asking: is the star on your forehead real?"

"Of course it's real!" Little Worm smiled.

"Can... can I touch it?" Butterfly stared at him mesmerized.

"Go ahead, my friend!" Little Worm encouraged him.

Before Little Worm had finished the sentence, Wind rushed forward and touched the star with the tip of his tail. Butterfly blushed and felt like apologizing for his friend, but Little Worm didn't seem to mind Wind's casual manner. Butterfly grinned and nodded, accepting the invitation: he felt Little Worm's mark on the forehead and tried gently rubbing out a corner. To his surprise, the slight pressure caused the mark to change color.

"Have you done that?" Butterfly asked Wind quickly.

"Nope!" Wind signed back putting his tail in the air to prove his innocence.

Dun-Bug shyly approached them, sat himself on a twig nearby and cleared his throat before speaking:

"I wish to thank you all for setting me free! I can't tell you how much this means to me! From today on, you are officially my favorite superheroes!" he declared.

"It was lucky we just happened to be around!" Cockerel modestly played it down.

"Lucky doesn't cut it! It was meant to be!" Butterfly spoke wisely. Everybody turned around to face him expecting an explanation.

"There is no such thing as good luck, bad luck or coincidence where I come from," Butterfly said briefly.

"Why not? What's wrong with those words?" Cockerel and duckling wanted to know more.

"Everything we say can become a self-fulfilling prophecy! We are brought up to believe that we need to fulfil our destiny which is set out for us before we were even born!" Butterfly told them.

"Who is setting out your destiny for you?" Cockerel wouldn't let it go.

"The powers that be!" Butterfly filled him in showing the sky with a theatrical gesture.

Dun-Bug was absent-mindedly listening from the side. Still shaken by what he had been through that day, his knees were discreetly knocking against one another. Little Worm noticed his distress and addressed him in a soft voice:

"Can I ask you something?"

"Anything!" Dun-Bug was pleased to see the others had already included him in their circle of friends.

"How did Mole manage to enslave you? I see you are very good on wings, unlike me…" Little Worm said.

Dun-Bug sighed heavily, and silence fell on them like a velvet curtain. Dun-Bug had everybody's undivided attention. He cleared his throat and started:

"I once saw a ladybug who made my heart race like nobody else had done before. Little did I know that love can account for some of the most disastrous decision one can make in his life… On that ill-fated day I threw myself into chasing after her, as I frantically picked up on the trail of her scent and rushed on like mad, forgetting all rational thought and behavior. After following her closely for the whole day, we finally reached a beautiful field full of blooming poppies at dusk. The scenery unfolding in front of us displayed such rare beauty; the stars flickering in the sky looked like they were whispering the untold secrets of heaven to the crimson-red flowers below. Magic was in the air…"

"Perhaps he was just dreaming…" Cockerel addressed Rica in a low voice.

Rica clasped his friend's beak between two fingers to shut him up: the poor soul in front of them had been through hell and back and Cockerel was being smart poking fun at him.

"The ladybug had landed on a fire-red rose majestically towering over the meadow like the conductor of a famous orchestra overseeing over a talented crowd of players... A warm feeling inside nudged me to give in to the ladybug's silent invite. Comfortably sitting against the bright red of the rose, she looked other-worldly beautiful to me: her long eyelashes languidly fluttering, her arm reaching out towards me... she never said a word, but I knew all she wanted was for me to join her and share that moment of heavenly peace in a tender embrace... A gentle breeze swayed the flowers back and forth scattering their scent all around... As I took my place next to her, I felt in perfect harmony with the universe... one flawless moment in time... I can't even describe it, words don't do it justice! What am I deluding myself about? If I were a poet or a painter I might be able to make you understand: our hands locking together, the fragrance of the meadow flowers mingling with the scent of my beloved made me wish I could hold onto that moment forever... That was her home and for a few blessed moments felt like mine, too... I closed my eyes surrendering to happiness..."

The power of the vivid memory transported him back in time. His words painted a picture which everybody present could relate to.

"What happened next?" Little Worm brought him back to where he'd left it.

"What happened next?" Dun-Bug nearly jumped out of his skin, his eyes wide open to look for his interlocutor.

"What happened? How did you end up like... that?" Little Worm gently nudged him in the right direction.

"It's not much more to say: I have no idea how long I drifted on dreaming hand in hand with my beloved, but I had a rude awakening finding myself tied up in ropes and hopelessly enslaved to Mole. You've all witnessed that sight, anyway..." Dun-Bug put a brief end to his story, slightly embarrassed. "Thank you so much to all of you for setting me free again!" he addressed the four friends.

"Are you seriously saying that we've set you free?" Cockerel replied rather surprised as he hadn't directly taken part in Dun-Bug rescue, busy as he was to find Little Worm.

"You have, indeed, given me back my freedom from that sly Mole, may he get as good as he gives!" Dun-Bug cursed Mole.

"Better to put it all behind you, my friend!" Little Worm advised wisely. "Paying back evil with evil makes you as bad as him!"

"Right you are! Don't let me stray away from the right path, little friend!" Dun-Bug smiled at Little Worm. "I have to admit that I remember catching a glimpse of Mole standing on the ground just underneath the rose. He was showering in the *dewdrops that fell off from the petals, but in my temporary madness, I chose to ignore the danger. Later on, when I woke up and I finally understood that the ladybug had vanished for good, it all became clear to me: the mesmerizing scenery, the magic and love in the air, the tantalizing scent of my beloved... everything turned out to be an illusion, or perhaps..."*

"*Or perhaps?*" Little Worm echoed his words with eager anticipation.

"*Or perhaps a well-put together trap... a figment of my imagination!*" Dun-Bug explained.

"*What have I told you? He's been dreaming a dream all along!*" Cockerel whispered triumphantly to Rica.

"Keep that beak of yours closed, or I'll close it for you. This little bug is holding nothing back from us, and you are having a laugh at his expense!" Rica told him off again.

"I should have remembered my granddad's advice; he always warned me to be watchful when love strikes because one can easily find himself a slave to his own feelings. I haven't listened to him, so I deserve everything I got. But from now on I'll be following his advice and I'll be much more sparing with those I trust in. As for my love-lust, I'll make sure that I keep that under control and keep my wits about me! I'll just let myself love another just enough to keep me going..." Dun-Bug concluded.

"Just enough to keep you going? Will you deny yourself ever being head over heels in love with someone from now on?" Cockerel couldn't believe his ears.

"He won't deny himself anything, just tone it down a bit: everything in moderation, a healthy dose of love will keep him going, without driving him off the rails!" Butterfly answered for Dun-Bug.

"Spot on!" Dun-Bug rejoiced at the thought someone understood him and approved of his thoughts. "Even to this day, I'm not sure whether it was love, infatuation or simply... stupidity on my part! But I know for sure that if it wasn't for you, I would still be a slave to Mole!"

"I think it's quite remarkable that you've managed to stay alive for so long!" Worm voiced out a thought that had been at the back of his mind for a while.

"Mole and I had an understanding!" Dun-Bug confessed.

"What kind of understanding?"

"I vowed that I would be his eyes every time he would come to surface!" Dun-Bug told them.

"What exactly were you supposed to do being Mole's eyes?" Little Worm asked on.

"I was supposed to guide Mole around while on the ground, and help him get his morning-dew showers, get his tan, get his whiskers tidy, things like these!" Dun-Bug mentioned a few of his jobs while in the service of Mole. "He has quite an austere and restrictive life down below, you know!"

"Speaking about the little jobs you had to do for Mole, I have one last question which you may find a bit uncomfortable, but I would appreciate your honest answer!" Worm quipped in a timid voice.

"Anything for you, my friend!" Dun-Bug reassured him.

"I can't stop thinking of that poor worm that Mole had for lunch... Have you, by any chance, helped Mole catch it?"

"Not at all!" Dun-Bug replied somewhat relieved. "My job today was to let Mole know well in advance of any threats and dangers coming our way! He was more

than capable of catching his own food relying on his sharp senses! You must have an idea of what I'm talking about!" Dun-Bug turned to Worm.

"Yep, I know everything there is to know on the topic!" Little Worm confirmed.

"That silly worm fell in the trap of his own accord today!" Dun-Bug commented with a streak of sorrow in his voice.

"How did it happen?" Cockerel looked for details as usual.

"Mole played a little recorder in to lure him in and eventually catch him. The strange thing is that the recorder had been crafted by someone belonging to the same species of worms as the one who fell victim to Mole today!" Dun-Bug commented expertly.

"How did Mole get hold of such a thing?"

"I couldn't tell you that because Mole had gotten hold of the recorder before he got hold of me, but one thing is for sure: he knew how to use it and he never hesitated to take full advantage of it. Unfortunately, the poor worm didn't stand a chance: the chilly morning fog together with the mesmerizing tune led him to an early tragic end!"

Cockerel stared at him in puzzlement; he could not see what the link was between the morning fog and the worm's awful death.

"Rule number one in a worm's survival skills is that you should never venture in open grounds on a foggy morning: the chill of the fog blunts down your senses and makes you an easy prey. But I'm a fine one to speak," Dun-Bug laughed at himself, "just like I had rushed in chasing after the ladybug, the worm followed the tune to his death! The naivety of youth... You live and learn, they say! That's if you survive it! But then you guys showed up from nowhere and Mole, in a fit of panic, threw the recorder at you..."

"Was that the recorder you are talking about?" Rica exclaimed just realizing what it was.

"Yes!" Dun-Bug nodded.

Wind hurried back to the spot where the recorder was still stuck in the ground at a slight angle. He swished swiftly through it and a random tune came out. Unsettled by the discovery, Wind joined his friends again.

"Crazy Mole... crazy like a fox!" Cockerel intervened. "Fancy hatching the sly plots he did: using somebody else's eyes to get you out and about, and luring in unknowing young worms by playing a tune on a recorder crafted by its own kind... You've got to give it to him, for all his faults, he was a clever old Mole! I wouldn't have thought that up in a million years!" Cockerel couldn't help admiring his ingenuity.

"You wouldn't have because you've got two good eyes and plenty of food to live on. Had you been blind and the food scarce and far in between, you would have come up with plenty of ideas, I bet!" Dun-Bug addressed him.

Cockerel had an idea: he closed his eyes, imagining he couldn't see anything. For a moment, the darkness and uncertainty around him frightened him out of his mind. He instantly opened his eyes again, unwilling to practice his imagination on those grounds any longer.

"I guess I should be wandering off now! It's about time I made an appearance back home. I've been missing a few days now and my family wouldn't have left many stones unturned looking for me! Many thanks again, I'll never forget what you've done for me today!"

Butterfly fluttered his wings and Wind curled up into a loop; they had been the rescuers and were modestly acknowledging Dun-Bug's gratitude.

"Besides, I've got a good lass waiting for me and I think many of the lads of my age are hoping I would never turn up to ask for her hand in marriage because she is a great catch for anyone! I must be a fool: I don't seem to see my luck for looking at it!"

Cockerel spanked his forehead.

"What's up with you?" the others cried out, unable to place his gestures in context.

"Are you kidding me? Have you heard that! He's got a lass soon-to-be-married to at home, but instead he eloped with a ladybug into a field full of poppies! Forget about the faithful girl waiting for you at home, forget about the fact that one poppy is enough for anyone to lose their minds, let alone a field full of them... Everything that happened to you, I call it moral justice!" Cockerel told him bluntly.

Dun-Bug wanted to reply, but Butterfly intervened saddened by his imminent departure:

"I was hoping you'd stick around for a bit longer, but I suppose everybody's got to take care of their own business..."

"Please don't say that!" Dun-Bug lowered his eyes.

"What else can I say when you've only been with us for a little while and ready to take off to greener pastures..." Butterfly scolded.

"I need to head back home as soon as possible to let everybody know I'm well and unharmed!"

Butterfly looked at his friends, but they all kept quiet.

"Very well, then... I just hope that we'll still get to see you now and again!" and his words were met with approving nods.

"Of course, of course... silly me! The honor and pleasure of being friends with you is all mine! You've saved my life today, and I count myself lucky to be your friend forever and ever!" Dun-Bug said in a trembling voice which echoed the trauma he had recently been through.

"Saved his life and freed him from bondage!" Cockerel whispered to Rica.

"How could I ever forget that? I'll always be your friend, Butterfly!" Dun-Bug pledged emotionally, ignoring the whispering that was going on between Rica and Cockerel.

"If you haven't noticed, not one word about returning the favor!" Cockerel carried on in a low voice.

"I won't hear another word!" Rica admonished him.

"I really have to go now!" Dun-Bug concluded firmly.

"Yeah, you go mind your own business, don't worry about us, your rescuers..." Cockerel drew Wind's attention by his mumbling.

"Thank for being so understanding and why don't we meet up tomorrow around lunchtime right here, under the bush?" Dun-Bug suggested.

"That's more like it! Why didn't he say that from the very beginning?" Cockerel tamed his tone.

Rica frowned at him and Cockerel winked mischievously.

"This spot will always have a special meaning in my mind as the crossroads of our destinies, the junction of fate which brought us all together today to seal our friendship forever!" Dun-Bug declared solemnly, making everybody stand tall and feel butterflies in their tummies.

"As far as I'm concerned, we can make this into a regular meeting place. I can easily fly my way in and out of here, if that's OK with everybody else!"

Rica, Cockerel, Butterfly and Wind peeked at one another.

"Considering that this spot was the house of horrors for you for a while, is it wise to keep coming back to it?" the duckling voiced out his concerns. "Why don't we meet up four bushes away from here?!"

The idea seemed to have caught with everybody, but Little Worm: the star on his forehead instantly lost its glow. Crawling as far as four bushes away from the spot was like a trip to the other side of the world for him, not to mention about the risks he exposed himself to during such a journey.

"There is no need to worry," Cockerel responded straight away to the change in Little Worm's mood. "I've got an offer that you can't refuse, I'll tell you all about it later!" Cockerel winked at him reassuringly.

Little Worm raised his brows in surprise, and the glow in his forehead mark came back.

"Remember that Mole's house lies beneath that oak leaf, and he has no intention of moving house soon!" Rica pleaded. "If you count four bushes going down the footpath in that direction," Rica continued, "We should be safe for regular meetings!"

Everybody agreed, except for Little Worm whose reservations lingered on. An almost imperceptible rustle tickled their ears, it was coming from the oak leaf and they all understood that Mole was listening to them. Revisiting the spot would have played straight into his hands!

"It's settled then: tomorrow at lunchtime, four bushes away from here!" they said, aware that being sparing on details would save them a future encounter with Mole.

They all watched the oak leaf trembling as Mole nuzzled it while finding out, with discontent, their change of plans.

Dun-Bug apologized for having to go so soon, thanked them again and off he flew to his family. Mole put his ear out hoping for some good news which would allow him to plan for a future happy meal! He was not brave enough to come out of his burrow for fear that the vulture could still be circling around the place.

After Dun-Bug lost himself in the distance, Cockerel turned his attention to Little Worm:

"My dear little friend, I've got an idea which is as exciting and unusual as our friendship: I'd like you to move in with me and my grandpa! I think it's a great idea, no need to thank me now, but you can if you insist! How about you come home with me today... I've got plenty of space, about this much and more!" Cockerel rumbled on excitedly, opening his wings to show everybody how large his house was.

"May you choke on your morning cry, you, filthy fowl!" Mole cursed from his burrow as he heard about the prospect of losing another meal.

"Do you want me to go home with you? What am I going to do there?" Little Worm's eyes bulged out of their sockets as details of his unexpected encounter with Cockerel from earlier that day flooded his mind.

If Little Worm hesitated taking up on Cockerel's suggestion, there was still hope for a meal...

"What do you mean what are you going to do there? Live there with granddad and me!" Cockerel continued as enthusiastically. "I understand you are an orphan now!"

"Maybe..." Little Worm was not convinced of Cockerel's rationale.

"What that maybe? Are you, or are you not an orphan?" Cockerel couldn't come to terms with Little Worm's indecisiveness.

"Are you asking me to become a member of your family?" Little Worm returned the question.

"I solemnly promise, I swear if you want me to, that I will never let any harm come to you..." Cockerel called out placing his right wing on his chest.

Little Worm fell quiet and sneaked a peek at a heap of half-dried leaves lying on the ground not far from where they were: for the untrained eye, they were just a cluster of leaves, but Butterfly understood right away what they were hiding. The intricate weaving of the twigs showing great care for the disposition of the leaves indicated that it was a home for a whole family of worms. It confirmed a suspicion that sprouted in Butterfly's mind when he heard a series of crystalline outbursts of laughter, while Dun-Bug was recounting the story of his imprisonment. At the time, Butterfly thought he just imagined it and didn't dare interrupt Dun-Bug, anyway.

Guessing what was on his friend's mind, Wind zipped off to the heap of leaves and peered under, confirming Butterfly's thoughts with a smile.

Little Worm picked up on their suspicions and wanted to block their way, but it was all too late: a whole family of little green worms with stars on their foreheads lived there! A mother, a father, grandparents, and two little girls, about the same age as Little Worm. Butterfly withdrew discreetly casting a meaningful glance in Rica's direction.

"Have you seen a ghost or something?" Rica questioned him jokingly.

Butterfly didn't say anything in case Mole would hear him, but after a few moments' thinking he flew over and lifted the heap of leaves just enough to let everybody see the family of worms whose forehead stars were going through all the colors of the rainbow, reflecting the strong emotions they were experiencing. Rica rubbed his eyes in disbelief: Little Worm mentioned nothing about his family to him! And to think that he saved from almost certain death in the first place!

Little Worm scribbled something on a leaf he found on the ground next to him and passed it on to Wind to carry it to Rica, who checked it out for a little while and smiled.

"Have a look at this, Butterfly!"

Butterfly hastened to check out the drawing which portrayed a flying cuckoo carrying in his beak a poppy-flower head out of which lots of little worms were sticking their heads out screaming in fear of their lives. Cockerel drew near pushed by curiosity but couldn't make head or tail of any of it.

"Little Worm didn't fall out of the sky on his own..." Rica explained to him.

"That makes sense... I was surprised to find that a teeny tiny worm knocked me out like that... Now, the lot of them being dumped on my head out of the blue, changes the situation completely!"

"Good point!" Rica agreed.

With that mystery solved, everybody turned their attention to the worm family.

"Good afternoon!" they greeted everybody in one voice.

Cockerel's intention of adopting Little Worm had suddenly become an unrealistic prospect since it came to light that the latter was not an orphan. But Cockerel was not one to give up easily!

"I know what we can do: I'll adopt all of you!"

Worm's parents looked at each other as if to tacitly agree on their reply, then said:

"We are staying here! All of us!" they said firmly.

Grandpa Worm stepped a few inches forward and took the floor.

"Don't take this the wrong way, my dear boy, but we can't come with you because this is our home now!" and he pointed at the cluster of leaves which sheltered them. "It was meant to be like this!"

His wise words implied that they were happy to go with the flow, take every opportunity and make the most of it.

"How can you say that this is your home when you are bamboo-worms and there is no such a thing as bamboo growing around here?" Cockerel asked confused.

Cockerel's comment didn't put off Grandpa Worm; with a broad smile on his face, he showed them a young plant:

"God has a plan for everyone!"

Cockerel glared at the long, thin stem of the young plant. "Well, well, I never…" his beak slack and his eyes wide open with amazement: a bamboo shoot had taken roots and was growing strong on the spot.

"I can see now why Mole chose to open up his burrow right here! He must have realized that the plant would soon attract one of the rarest species of worms that there is! He's not stupid!" Cockerel spoke his mind out.

"You've got that one right, my winged friend!" Grandpa Worm praised him.

The four friends took turns to check out, feel, and smell the bamboo shoot as they had never seen one before.

"You can understand now why we can't go with you. We've got everything we need here; the young plant provides us with a home and food which we otherwise wouldn't get much of in this part of the world."

"What about Mole? Won't he be a constant danger for you all? He is sly and sharp on his senses; you've heard what happened to Dun-Bug and the poor worm he gobbled up for lunch. What will you do if he comes after you?" Cockerel finally talked about his main concern.

Grandma Worm stepped out of ranks and addressed Cockerel in a gentle voice:

"You and your friends have already taken care of that for us without even realizing: moles are a proud kind who never go back to a place of defeat no matter what! If they think their life is in danger, they are out of there for good!"

"What's that got to do with Mole here?" Cockerel couldn't see the connection.

"The news of a predator circling up in the sky has made quite an impression on him today!"

"I beg your pardon?" Cockerel seemed surprised at the news himself and slipped a quick peek at the sky from under his brows.

"You and your friends managed to fool him good and proper today. Mole certainly didn't like the idea of a vulture hunting him down from the sky! He'll never come to the surface again in this spot, that's for sure!" Grandma Worm exclaimed with a smile. "But full of grudge as he is, he might try to hoax other moles into resurfacing here in order to put an early end to their lives!"

"Suppose for a moment he does come back," Cockerel didn't budge, "after all, Mole is a creature of habit who likes his comforts. He's left behind this wonderfully smooth stone, his favorite sun bed. I bet that's been brought here from a great distance to provide him with plenty of moments of rest and relaxation!" Cockerel argued his point.

"That smooth stone you are talking about provided him with a lot more than rest and relaxation in the sun," Grandma Worm told them.

"What else did the stone do for him?" Cockerel couldn't help himself.

"It allows him to put his feet up and be off the ground for a while!" Grandma Worm filled them in.

"Why is that so important?"

"When you take your weight off your feet, they say, you add on days to your life!" Grandma Worm informed them.

Through a quick exchange of glances Rica and Cockerel agreed on the questionable nature of that statement, but they would never in a million years dispute an old lady's words of wisdom!

Butterfly noticed their silent understanding and smiled; he knew exactly what Grandma Worm meant.

"If that's true, how come that your life is so short?" Cockerel burst out before Rica could nudge him to silence.

"Hey, you are getting into a bad habit!" Cockerel told him off rubbing his wing. "I just wanted to point out how naïve Mole can be, that's all!"

"Why do you think he is naïve?" Grandma accepted his challenge.

"How can he believe something like that? Ha-ha-ha!" Cockerel laughed out loud.

"Children, you should never underrate naivety. It is the one trait of character which allows us to look at the world around with wonder and renewed hope, and it gives us the resilience to start everything all over again... In fact, our naivety is our only excuse and the very reason why we are being tolerated..."

"By whom?" Cockerel asked.

"By the Holy One, of course, who is beyond and above the whole creation and life itself!" Grandma Worm explained.

Butterfly nodded approvingly, and Cockerel fell silent. Grandma Worm let off a sigh as she cast a loving glance over her family.

"Your thoughtful proposition is very much appreciated, but you really don't need to worry about us; Mole can't reach us on the branches up high. For a start, he would have to keep himself safe from the razor-sharp thorns of the mulberry bush growing around the bamboo shoot!" Father Worm pointed out confidently

The four friends only had to take a closer look to convince themselves of the truth Father Worm's words carried.

"God willing, we'll be able to keep our wits about us, unlike Dun-Bug who was easily led! Besides, we weren't all born yesterday!" Father Worm alluded to the good mix of generations in their family.

"Weren't you!?" Cockerel exclaimed rather surprised; until then, all worms had been the same to him; a delicious snack as individuals, and a hearty meal when they came in families! But this time Cockerel meant no harm and would have gladly taken in the whole worm family, had there been a need for it!

From under the oak leaf, Mole was still listening, and nearly screamed in anger listening to such an accurate assessment of his situation. Instead, he bit his finger with spite, imagining he stuck his fangs into a juicy worm! He suspected something else was going on under that bush. His mastermind plan had been to enslave Dun-Bug and train him to guide raids on small creatures like those worms. Luckily for everybody else but Mole, it all went pear-shaped and not many were harmed!

"Worm, you are old enough now to keep yourself safe and sound, so why not join us in our adventures," Cockerel tempted him opening his wings wide. "I'm sure we'll come across another bamboo shoot somewhere, and if not, I can always ferry you back and forth. I'm sure your family won't say no to it!" Cockerel pushed the envelope.

Rica edged closer to Cockerel and nudged him again drawing his attention to Worm's sisters who had flanked their brother on both sides, both locking hands with him as if to show they didn't approve of such an idea. The sight of the three siblings standing together like one, finally brought it home for Cockerel: he had been selfish in putting forward that suggestion! He quickly changed the subject, trying to mend the damage.

"Don't mind me babbling on, what I meant to say is that we'll keep in touch and I'll call in now and again to see how you are!"

"He means we'll all call in to see you every so often!" Butterfly corrected him.

"That's exactly right! Shall we say… tomorrow at lunch time as we've already established with Dun-Bug?" Cockerel chirped enthusiastically. "Are your family OK with it as well? We'd hate to impose on you!" Cockerel added quickly, eager to show he had taken on board Rica's warnings.

"Not at all, you are welcome anytime!" the whole family answered in one voice.

"You can tell us how Cuckoo got hold of you!" Rica suggested excited at the idea of a story.

"It's a date then!" Little Worm quipped happily.

They said their goodbyes as Cockerel, Rica, and Butterfly walked from under the bush into the open road. Wind hesitated to follow them for a few moments; he was flying this way and that way, keeping an eye on spying Mole beneath the oak leaf. He eventually swished off after his friends to let Butterfly know about his worries.

Butterfly fell quiet for a few seconds while his eyes were wandering around the place as if looking for something specific. Suddenly, his stare lingered over Mole's smooth stone and his friends could tell he had an idea. Rica and Cockerel took one look at the smooth stone shinning in the sun and they instantly knew what Butterfly was thinking: cover the opening of Mole's burrow with the stone.

"Why not!" they both voiced out a rhetorical question.

"This way we'll make sure that Mole could never come to surface again on the spot and our friend's family will be safe from him!" Butterfly argued the case.

No sooner said and done! Cockerel and Rica joined their forces and after a strain, a push, and a shove, they managed to cover the entrance to Mole's burrow. Mole, who was following everything from the other side of the oak leaf, was seething with anger.

"Thank you all for your kindness!" the worms called out.

"The pleasure is all ours!" Rica, Cockerel, Butterfly and Wind called back.

Mole was cursing them dead, but nobody cared about him any more: out of sight is out of mind after all! The four little adventurers were ready to set out again, when Wind beckoned Butterfly to grab the recorder thrown at them earlier by Mole.

"You're right!" Cockerel agreed picking up the recorder and pursing his lips to blow in it. In an instant, Rica reached out and snatched the instrument from his friend.

"What's gotten into you?" Cockerel snapped at him.

"I'm trying to spare us any unwanted attention!" Rica whispered cautiously.

"In this case, I'll postpone it for later!" Cockerel conceded smilingly.

"Suit yourself, my friend!" Rica smiled back.

They had only set foot on the path when some crackling noises from the bush made them turn their heads. Little Worm was seeing them off from a leaf up high. As they turned around, they saw Worm flushed up, his hands covering his behind and the tip of his tail poking at the stem of the leaf as if to deflect attention from something else. Rica remembered what the noises were, and a smile blossomed in the corner of his mouth.

"What's up with him now?" Cockerel wondered.

"Why don't you give him the recorder as a token of our friendship?" Rica suggested.

"Are you serious?" Cockerel seemed taken aback by the proposal.

"It's no use to us, unless you are thinking of luring in innocent victims like Mole used to do!" Rica challenged him directly.

Cockerel breathed in deeply; it felt rather uncomfortable as he stood there with all of them awaiting his decision.

"I agree with Rica!" Butterfly increased the pressure.

"All right, you win!" Cockerel gave in. "There you are, Little Worm, it belongs to you by right!" Cockerel handed over the recorder to his little friend.

"Thank you a thousand times!" Little Worm received the unexpected present with great delight and squeezed it to his chest.

"Well, see you tomorrow!" they all waved at Little Worm.

They walked in silence for a while, until they reached a crossroads.

"From here on I have to go that way!" Butterfly let his friends know showing them the path on the right.

Cockerel was taken by surprise, stopped briskly, and stared in the direction pointed out by Butterfly.

"And I have to go that way!" Rica said showing them the path on the left.

Cockerel shuffled from one leg to the other, a bit unsettled in himself.

"Why are you so frisky? Have you seen something?" the others took notice of his unrest.

"If it's not too much to ask, duckling, can I walk home with you? This way, we'll keep each other company and I'll get to see where about you live!" Cockerel muttered in a low voice.

"But why go to such a length since tomorrow we'll see each other again?" Rica replied.

"Just trying to make sure you get home safe and sound. I've got plenty of time and the sun is still up in the sky, so…" Cockerel made it up as he went along.

Rica and Butterfly peeked at each other: neither of them had bought Cockerel's shaky excuse.

"OK, OK … I wanted to find out where you live… Happy now!" Cockerel admitted.

"Why is that such a big deal to you?" Rica and Butterfly questioned him in unison.

"What if you can't make for tomorrow's playdate? I'd like to know where I can find you…" Cockerel mumbled, and his friends could sense panic in his voice.

"But why would you think that I wouldn't make it for tomorrow's playdate?" Rica tried to get to the bottom of Cockerel's distress.

"I don't know... I'm always assuming that things can go wrong for a variety of reasons... Look at us today, for instance: we've been through so much since we met... You never know what the next day brings on..." Cockerel said a bit embarrassed by his own behavior. In his defense, however, no child could have gone through what he had and remain untouched by the fear of losing loved ones.

"What exactly are you trying to say?" Butterfly insisted as he loathed the idea of leaving his friends less than happy.

"I don't know... Say a rain drop knocks you out and the blow to the head erases any memories of me as your friend..." he voiced out but one of the many fatalist ideas buzzing through his head.

Rica, Butterfly and Wind involuntarily stared at the sky at the same time, causing Cockerel to feel increasingly awkward in himself.

"Sorry, guys, I guess it was the wrong choice of words: let's just say that I hope whatever happens it would be a stroke of luck, rather than a blow to the head, or at least a lucky blow to the head like in Worm's case!" Cockerel tried to cheer up the mood.

"Don't get me wrong, my friend," Rica felt obliged to explain his reaction, "I have no problem showing you where I live if you have the time to spare, and quite honestly, I could do with some company on the way home..."

"Now you're talking! I always have time to spare for a good friend! We better be on our way!" Cockerel laughed

"We know where the duckling lives!" Butterfly giggled while playing tag with Wind, who was ruffling their feathers getting really close to their skin and giving them a chill just for a laugh.

When they eventually arrived in front of the gate, they all stopped.

"Well, that explains why you decided to run away from home; one look at your sisters' fancy hats, and you're on your way out of here!" Cockerel commented sympathetically winking at Rica. "How did your sisters get hold of those hats?"

"They made them out of flower petals," Butterfly answered for Rica. "They must have been inspired by my suggestions! Think of it: they've created a new fashion trend and I helped them do it!"

"You and your pranks!" Rica smiled. "It's like the angel in my shadow!" Rica remembered and raised his wings above his shoulder to recreate the silhouette of an angel.

"Very much so: I rested on their beaks, then on their heads and they soon came up with the idea..."

"So, you are saying you are at the heart of this?" Rica looked at him from the side.

"I'm not just saying it, it's the truth!" Butterfly exclaimed. Then, watching the sun getting close to the horizon, he added:

"It's about time I wandered off in the horizon…"

"And where exactly is off in the horizon?" Rica and Cockerel became curious.

"I have a lovely ladybird waiting for me somewhere in the cup of a flower. I bumped into her while watching you from afar talking to Cuckoo and Magpie…" Butterfly confessed.

"You met your girlfriend while spying on him?" Cockerel couldn't believe what he was being told.

"Yes, I was hiding in the cup of a flower for my own safety!" Butterfly defended himself.

Wind whooshed through the surrounding vegetation and then back to Butterfly: his friend was not as truthful as usual.

"OK, OK, if you must go into the tiniest details, it was more of a coincidence than a planned encounter!" Butterfly admitted.

"More details, more details!" Rica and Cockerel urged him joining their voices.

"While trying to locate the duckling again, Wind was giving me a piggy-back ride and stopped abruptly when he caught sight of our friend here chatting away with Cuckoo. As you would expect, I came rolling off straight into a flower cup…"

"When did all of these happen?" Rica frowned.

"You were busying yourself talking to Cuckoo, like I've just said!" Butterfly replied slightly irritated at the duckling's lack of attention.

"Well, when you put it this way, it looks like you've taken refuge in the flower cup rather than hidden away to spy on me!"

"If you like it better, so be it: I took refuge, not hidden!" Butterfly agreed appealingly.

"I do like it better, indeed!" Rica smiled pleased with the outcome of his finding, as the last thing he would have liked to come to light was him being spied on by one of his friends. "But still, a question remains: why did you do it?"

"Remember Dun-Bug and Mole, I could have been in the same situation if Cuckoo had gotten hold of me!" Butterfly explained.

"Oh, no!" Cockerel couldn't stifle his outrage.

"What now?" the others turned around.

"Are you saying that you've made another good friend today while trying to keep yourself safe and sound?" Cockerel spelt it out for them.

"You could say that," Butterfly confirmed, himself amazed at that revelation.

"In this case, why don't you invite the ladybug to meet all of us tomorrow at lunch-time and join our friendship circle?" Cockerel suggested.

"Should I? But why?" Butterfly didn't quite understand where Cockerel was coming from.

"But why not?" Cockerel replied promptly. "In a circle of friends, the more, the merrier!" Cockerel explained to him. "We were saying today that good friends share food, water, clothes, and good spirits! The only thing we don't share is..."

"What is that?"

"Romantic love, of course!" Cockerel smiled.

"Of course, of course!" Butterfly understood straight away. "On that note, I will say goodbye now to all of you and look forward to seeing you tomorrow. If Ladybug so wishes, I'll invite her along, too!" Butterfly promised.

"Why would she turn down meeting us? Is she one of those smug girls?" Cockerel was getting a bit worried,

"Not at all! It's just a way of saying!" Butterfly reassured him.

Butterfly opened his wings ready to take off, when Cockerel reached out to him, stalling his departure.

"One last thing..."

"What is it now?" Butterfly stopped in his tracks.

"What direction are you flying off?"

"Why are you asking?" Butterfly was taken aback by Cockerel's interest in such things.

"We might have the same way, in which case we can postpone a bit the split up!" Cockerel confessed.

Butterfly looked this way and that way, and said decisively:

"I'm flying that way!" and he indicated the direction of flight.

"Brilliant!" Cockerel rejoiced. "I'm going that way, too!" Then they both turned to Rica and bid him goodbye, setting out on their way.

Rica saw them off until they vanished in the distance. Then he turned to face the gate of his parents' house with a heavy heart; he opened it and stepped into the front garden, but as he did so a strong cheesy smell hit him. He stared down at the ground, where the stench was coming from, and realized that his feet were still soiled in bird dropping from earlier on in the day. He walked out of the front garden and wiped his feet on a wilting plant nearby, which cheered up straight away. Rica found it difficult to face the sad reality at home after such an interesting day out, so he delayed as much as possible to get back in. He went around collecting dewdrops to wash his feet. Then he picked up some pollen and sprinkled it all over himself, and last but not least, he tidied up his quiff. He checked his own reflection in a dewdrop, but there were no signs that the beauty spot gifted to him by Mother Swallow would come in sight any time soon. He let out a heavy sigh, and finally opened the front gate with a brisk gesture meant to attract his sisters' attention. But it was to no avail, the girls were marching on regardless; none of them saw him, nor did they hear the loud bang of the gate closing behind Rica. It was as if he didn't even exist! They kept cat-walking, imagining they were performing on the greatest stage in the world.

Defeated, Rica caved in, surrendering to the harsh reality in front of him. He sat himself on the bench placed near a shrub. An old dragonfly was resting on a leaf, watching her younger friends cheering and applauding the ducklings' show. Just then, the sharp screech of the front gate opening drew everybody's attention.

Many of the small insects who had been part and parcel of the show until then, acting as broaches or even clip-on earrings, became alert and whispered in the ducklings' ears:

"Somebody's just come through the gate! Better check out who that is!"

This time it was the parents arriving home, making an awful lot of noise as they said goodbye to a big crowd of birds carrying on their way home to their young. The ducklings put a brief end to their fashion show and hurried off the catwalk to welcome their parents. A swarm of elderly insects dozing off in the sun started applauding automatically, thinking the ducklings were taking a short break to rest. Then they dopily looked around for their grandchildren who had been the heart and soul of the lively audience of the improvised fashion show.

"Is that all for today?" they checked out with their off-spring the entertainment schedule for the day.

The ducklings made their way to their parents, keeping up their fashion icon demeanor. Both parents dropped off their luggage and opened their arms to cuddle their beloved daughters.

"Look at you, the most beautiful ducklings on earth!" they said admiringly, like all parents do.

The girls huddled up in their parents' embrace, while Rica watched from his bench. The swarm of young and old insects sighed in relief that the hullaballoo was over for the day. Although the hatchlings were greatly entertained by such shows, their parents and grandparents secretly worried that it might have been a bad influence on them.

"Thank goodness it's all over for today!" the elderly murmured in their wisdom.

Sadder than ever, Rica stood up and went into the house closing the door behind him.

"But where is your little brother?" he heard his father's voice.

The girls' chuckles and giggles stopped for a moment, as they spared a moment of their precious time looking around for their little brother. As if to make a point, the door of the house opened on its own with a cringy screech. It must have been a mischievous gust of wind eager to nose through the house; it had made its way in through the window but couldn't trace its way back out and decided to burst out with a push of the door. The loud protest of the door being forced open unexpectedly drew everybody's attention.

Father Duck walked into the house to look for his only son and called out shortly from inside:

"Relax, everybody! He's here!"

"Here is my little prince!" Mother Duck burst out relieved. "I'd like to know straight away what's turned my handsome, bright yellow prince into a blue little grump!" Mother Duck joked attempting to put a smile on Rica's face.

"Oh, it's nothing, Mom! Really, nothing!" Rica made an effort to appear casual and light-hearted, thinking to himself that it was no point in ruining his parents' day with his silliness.

"You must tell your mom the truth, my darling! I can see you are not your usual happy self, so it must be something bothering you! You know you can tell me anything!" Mother Duck insisted.

"It's nothing to worry about, Mom, honestly!" Rica played it down.

But Rica's parents were not to be so easily persuaded that their instincts were wrong. In the end, Rica cracked:

"I wish my sisters weren't such hard work! I'm getting sick and tired of their attitude!" he complained.

"Oh, so that's the problem!" the parents locked eyes and nodded at each other understandingly.

They cuddled and kissed Rica and all of a sudden, things didn't seem as grim. The candlelight bobbed up and down approvingly.

"I didn't tell you in the first place because I didn't want to spoil your happiness! I'd like to see you happy and cheerful all the time!" Rica whispered cuddling up to her, as he touched the beauty spot on her cheek.

All of a sudden the door was slammed against the wall and the girls burst inside, each trying to get closer to Mom and Dad for a hug.

"You stay here with him and I'll go to the kitchen to cook dinner!" Mother Duck instructed her husband.

"We'll come with you, Mom!" the girls flocked into the kitchen behind Mother Duck.

Even then, they ignored Rica busy to keep up with the crowd and not miss out on anything. At last alone with Rica, Father Duck told him:

"It's only you and I left here, nobody can hear us. What's on your mind, Son?"

Rica didn't need much persuasion to open up to his dad; he told him about all the things that upset him.

"If there is one piece of advice I would give you on this is that you shouldn't take to heart the silliness of your sisters."

"But, Dad, you don't understand! They keep ignoring me and I don't seem to be able to get in their good books, no matter what! How can you defend them? Are you on their side, too?" Rica replied begrudgingly.

"Dear boy, you'll understand these things better as you grow up... As you advance in age, your outlook on life will change..." Father Duck soothed him with a gentle stroke on the head.

Rica looked down at his feet, being the first thing which came to mind when he thought of advancing... But his father tapped his head gently and said:

"Your feet help you advance on the road outside our house and get where you want to be, but your mind will help you advance in understanding things about yourself and others, and it will help you conquer obstacles, turn hardships and mistakes into a learning experience. As you grow up, your set of values will change, and you will get to reassess your judgments as a child..." Father Duck tried his best to explain.

"I don't understand!" Rica admitted.

"Think about the stars in the sky: when you are a child, they spark magic and mystery in your life, but as you grow up you get to see them in a different light!" Father Duck pleaded.

"I kind of see what you mean, but can you give me another example?" Rica became interested in the topic.

"Let's take, for example, the role of the parents for their children: in your early childhood, your parents are the pillars of your world. They might not be as you wanted them to be, nevertheless, you love them dearly and wouldn't change them for the world! You look up to them and they become your heroes in many ways!"

"They are, aren't they?" Rica agreed looking at the image of St George wrestling the dragon which was hanging on the wall of the living room.

"I have to tell you that the way you view your parents as a young child will dramatically change during the time of your life: they tend to lose the heroic glamour, as well as their authority..." Father Duck revealed.

"But why?" Rica couldn't get his head around it.

Because you gain your independence and that, like everything in life, has a price!" Father Duck smiled.

"But why?" Rica made an effort to take in every word.

"Because personal independence enables you to gain your own set of values and to judge everything on their own merits!"

"Dad, I don't get it!" Rica whispered almost in tears.

"When you become your own person, you'll most likely want to leave behind many of the things you had grown fond of in your childhood and replace them with something else, something which you think is better."

Rica said nothing, but his eyes kept questioning.

"If you take a look at the continents of the world, you'll find that each of them holds a secret longing for the others, as they all used to belong to the same gigantic sheet of land, but in separating from one another, they each got to be independent and established their own identity... In the same way, you and your sisters will be grown-ups one day and won't need the support of your parents... and, between you and me, that's not such a bad thing; as they grow old, parents become nagging and moody sometimes..."

Rica nearly choked and had to cough loudly to clear the knot in his throat.

"But as parents grow old, children grow up and take their rightful place in the world, fulfilling their destiny..."

"How am I going to fulfil my destiny?" Rica asked with a streak of fear in his voice.

"You'll be a father one day, and decide you want to do things differently from your parents; you'll bring up your children in your own way, you'll live your life according to your own principles and you'll decide to love some people more than others... For you must know one thing: there is only so much love you can spread around, and you'll have to be wise in who you choose to love... The love you have for your parents as a child, will later on be shared amongst your best friends and family!"

Rica pondered over his father's words which sounded all big and complicated.

"I know it's hard to understand at your age, but think of how your mother and I try to give you and your sisters the best we can: the best food, the best clothes... This is the kind of love which will stay with you for the rest of your life, even when you are a grown-up yourself with your own family; and you will do the same with your children!" Father Duck tried to break it up to Rica's level of understanding.

But after battling all those complicated thoughts for a while, Rica did what any child would: he jumped on his dad's knees and locked his hands around him squeezing with all the might of his love for his dad.

"Dad, I'll never love you less, and that's a promise!" he breathed out his words.

Father Duck welled up; he could remember clearly a similar scene between himself and his father who was now just a memory. Father Duck hugged Rica back and spoke out reassuringly:

"It's OK, Son, you should know that I'll never love you less, either! And you should never be afraid to love those who are worthy of your love, because love makes the world go around!"

Gently disengaging Rica's arms from around his shoulders, Father Duck said looking his son in the eye:

"Coming back to your sisters, now, you should not bear grudge against them because they are so airy-fairy and so carried away doing their own thing!"

"Even if that upsets me?" Rica replied.

"It upsets you now, because you are little, and they are not much older, either. They are now very young and carefree; they see themselves as the center of their own world, and therefore nothing and no one can distract them from having fun and playing. But in time, your relationship with your sisters will change, and you will all look back at these times and laugh together about it all! Besides, there will come a time when somebody else will take central stage in your life, and at that point you won't want to spend that much time with your sisters, while they'll be looking for your company more and more."

Rica stared at his dad in disbelief.

"Mark my words and cherish this time, because it will never come back!" Father encouraged him.

"Won't it?" was all Rica could mutter under his breath.

"Your sisters will grow up: they might look like the spoilt daughters of destiny at the moment, riding high on the wave, but they'll soon have to change places and be the ones working hard to keep the wave going. That's never easy, as life can be full of surprises, and not all of them are pleasant!" Father Duck told Rica who was getting ready to throw in a comment but decided to wait and see what his dad would tell him next.

"I know you don't understand everything I'm telling you today, but remember our little chat and trust me, because it will all come to pass one day!" Father Duck sealed his promise with a little tap on Rica's nose.

"Do you think that my sisters will change their ways as they grow up and start treating me better?" Rica asked for clarification.

Dad met his demands with a smile and a nod.

"Not only will they treat you better, but you'll have a special place in their hearts! Think about it: you are their only little brother, you'll be to them as special as a shooting star falling from the sky."

"How rare is a shooting star falling out of the sky?" Rica wanted to know.

"Very rare, indeed! Not everybody gets to see one during their lifetime, let alone have one as a brother!" Father Duck joked.

"Why is it that not many get to see one during their lifetime?"

"Because all shooting stars come from the garden of heaven and the only way one can get there is either by an effort of imagination, or in a dream!" Father Duck carried on.

Suddenly, Rica felt at peace with everything and travelled back in time remembering the events of the day which played in his mind like a film: his encounter *with Butterfly, then Cockerel and the rescue of the baby swallow… It all felt like a dramatic dream with a happy ending.*

The door of the room opened with a screech of hinges and a young voice announced:

"Dinner is served!"

"Not a minute too soon!" Father Duck exclaimed watching the last rays of sun dying out below the horizon. Then he took Rica's hand and they both went into the kitchen where they had dinner with everybody else.

After that, the sisters went off to meet their friends in the village and tell them all about the catwalk and the excitement of new fashion trends.

The dark fell over the village like a heavy velvet curtain. Grasshoppers started their nocturnal tunes, performed from their favorite hiding places, the cups of evening primroses! Thus, for the rest of the evening Rica's family enjoyed their music till it was time for bed. Shortly before they settled in for the night, Father Duck had a little word with his wife about Rica. Mother Duck nodded her head and later on that night, when she tucked all the children in bed, she fussed about Rica a bit more than usual.

"How about mommy sleeps with you tonight, my darling?" she suggested in a whisper.

Rica's face lit up in a broad smile as he shuffled to the far side of the bed to make room for his mom.

"What about us? We want to sleep with you, as well!" the sisters protested feeling a bit jealous of their little brother.

"Wait for your turn tomorrow night!" Mother Duck told them.

Then Mother Duck cuddled up her baby son and gave him a kiss on the right cheek where Mother Swallow placed the magic drop. Rica hugged his mom tight and went to sleep very quickly.

Next day in the morning, Rica was on his own in the bed when he woke up. In fact, as he got out of bed, he realized he was on his own in the house. Crystal clear outbursts of laughter coming from outside indicated that his sisters were back at playing their favorite game. Again!

"I will never understand how they do the same thing over and over again, and don't get fed up with it!" Rica slapped his forehead.

The fashion show of the day was in full swing and a whole swarm of insects were flying around cheering on and applauding frantically. It's always the way with the free of charge shows.

"I've got a playdate to make it to today," Rica reminded himself as he recounted in his mind the adventures of the previous day.

He checked out the position of the sun in the sky and sighed with relief; still plenty of time! It was only mid-morning. Rica went and picked up a clean change of clothes from his wardrobe which his mom had left for him and grabbed his favorite towel with red hearts on his way out. He peeked through the net curtains outside at his sisters, before he opened the door and let it close behind with a loud bang. As usual, the noise got no reactions from his sisters who were far too engrossed in their pretend catwalk.

He marched across the front garden to the shower cabin which Father Duck put up for the use of the family during summer. It was a clever installation in the middle of a rose bush skilfully crafted to collect the night dew and turn it into scented water by morning. It was just enough for Rica to have a refreshing bath that would set him up for the day. After a thoroughly enjoyable dip, Rica dried himself and put on fresh clothes. He then picked up the comb to tidy up his quiff and turn around to find a big enough dewdrop which would mirror back his reflection. But no sooner did he look at himself in the make-shift mirror, and he froze on the spot. The sudden stiffness which got hold of his body made his backbone crackle, while his heart raced like mad! A few bees buzzed around interested to find out what was going on."

"Why did the duckling freeze on the spot, Mom?" I burst out impatiently.

"Why do you think? The beauty spot gifted by Mother Swallow had finally become his own for good! It was on his right cheek, where his mom had kissed him the night before, and it was shining like a star in the night sky!" my mom explained.

"Really?" I whispered with a knot in my throat, touching my own beauty spot on the right cheek.

"I thought you might like that…" Mom winked at me.

"Rica felt his cheek in disbelief: it didn't come off! Just like Mother Swallow had promised, the beauty spot was there to stay, and more importantly, it was his!

Rica started jumping up and down with excitement attracting everybody's attention upon himself: all insects big and small swarmed in towards him, leaving behind the fashion parade of his sisters, as well as the older insects who had dozed off in the meantime.

"What's up? What's going on?" the insects asked one another while making their way to Rica.

"The beauty spot!"

"The beauty spot? What beauty spot are we talking about now?"

"Look at the beauty spot on the duckling's cheek! It shines like a star on a clear summer night and I reckon the little duckling must have done something amazing to have earned it!" the insects changed opinions amongst themselves.

The word about Rica's beauty spot soon got around and stirred such a great racket.

"A miracle, a miracle has just happened!" they were sharing the news amongst themselves.

In no time, Rica's sisters were left with no audience. Even the insects who acted as accessories for their fancy dress show dropped everything and flew off. The complete desertion was beyond belief for Rica's sisters; exchanging outraged glances, they decided that instance to go and see for themselves how and why Rica managed to upstage them. They waddled as fast as their feet took them to the rose bush where Rica was standing, watching mesmerized his new beauty spot.

"Where is that coming from? How did he get it?" they kept asking one question after another.

Resourceful as she was, the oldest sister took out of her handbag a little mirror and an eyeliner and dotted a beauty spot on her right cheek, an almost perfect copy-cat of Rica's. After giving herself a beauty spot, she let out a lady-like cough to attract her sisters' attention. Turning their heads quickly from Rica to their eldest sister, the others noticed that there was no shine to the latter's beauty spot. Still, they were interested to find out how she managed to get one of those for herself so quickly.

"How did you get that?" they questioned her.

The eldest sister put out her mirror and eyeliner. The reflection of the sun in the pocket mirror blinded them for a moment.

"Yours is not shiny like his!" they noticed.

The eldest sister burst into laughter.

"You wait!" she answered confidently, as she dipped a finger in her own saliva and dabbed the beauty spot turning her face to the sun. Her beauty spot was now shining bright.

The demonstration had been enough for the others: they all produced pocket mirrors as well as eyeliners out of their handbags and started crafting their own beauty spots and perfecting them with a shiny finishing touch. They all marched back to their improvised stage, convinced that they had managed to catch up on the latest trend and get back on track with their fashion show. They walked up and down the stage, expecting the insects, their loyal followers, to swarm in any moment. But no matter how hard they tried, it never happened! Besides, their beauty spots were no match for Rica's: as soon as the moisture dried up, they became dull. Intrigued at their fans' indifference, one of the sisters went over to a cluster of small insects who had never missed a show before and pleaded with them:

"Gather around and watch our best show so far!"

The insects, however, wouldn't budge! Seeing there was no way of winning their audience over on the back of glory past, one of the sisters edged towards Rica and when she was close enough, she reached out trying to smudge off the beauty spot on his face, as she couldn't bring herself to believe that her little brother's mark was genuine and not painted on like theirs. Very much to the sisters' surprise, the beauty spot not only did not wipe out, but it kept its shine!

"What kind of ink have you used, brother?" she asked whisperingly, employing as much discretion for fear she might lose face in front of the insects.

"I haven't used any ink!" Rica replied taken aback by her reaction.

"You've done without any ink?" his sister's jaw fell slack as the petals adorning her forehead became dislodged and floated quietly to the ground, which started a wave of giggles and chuckles amongst the old insects; they were enjoying the awkwardness of the situation as much as their grandchildren used to enjoy the fashion shows!

"How can you do this to me?" Rica's sister lamented. "We are your sisters, the same flesh and blood, and as loyal to you as the stars are to the moon! Are you trying to shame us beyond repair in front of our fans? What have we ever done to you to deserve this!" she carried on with the drama. "Girls, you better come and see this!" she called out to the others.

They all responded to the call like one, gathering around Rica, in an attempt to block out the swarm of insects who stayed put, ready to pick up on any word, any gesture, any comment.

"Mark my words, this lad might just be the one to teach these little madams a good lesson!" one of the elder insects prophesized.

"They could learn one or two things on humility and wisdom!" another one remarked.

Upon seeing their die-hard fans being so outspoken in their criticism of them, Rica's sisters were panic-stricken.

"I'm telling you the truth," Rica argued his case from their midst, "my beauty spot is not fake, it's genuine!"

The insects stopped their giggling at once, and one of them unwarily managed to catch a ray of sunshine in her long ropy eyelashes. Hit by the double whammy of Rica's revelation and their peer's unprecedented success, the insects were bobbing their heads trying to keep an eye on Rica and the sunray catcher at the same time; it was hard work for such small creatures!

To everybody's amazement, the sunray catcher ignored her own success, looking rather bored and gloomy as she threw in a comment:

"Don't judge them too harshly, they are young and naïve!"

In the meantime, the sisters huddled up on Rica, immobilizing him: they sheltered his face from the sun in the hope that the beauty spot would stop shining, they searched his pockets thoroughly for the mystery paint responsible for the spectacular visual effect, they even rubbed his cheek as hard as they could trying to make it disappear! Nothing happened, apart from Rica becoming really distressed and freaked out by his out-of-control sisters.

"Ouch! You are hurting me! If you don't stop right now whatever you are doing, I'm telling Mom and Dad!" Rica cried out in desperation.

"It does look genuine…" the sisters concluded. "But how can that be? Perhaps an angel from the heaven called in last night and bestowed a blessing upon him while we were all asleep!" one of them ventured an idea.

"Why do you think it was last night and not in the morning?" the others argued the point.

"Girls… have you noticed something?" the one above them drew their attention.

"Noticed what?" the others turned their attention to her,

"Our little brother had just had his morning bath…" she followed up on her idea.

"So?" the others couldn't understand where she was going with it.

"Perhaps this is where he encountered the angel!" she suggested proud of her logic.

"But we were on the exact same spot much earlier this morning!" the others protested at the idea. "He was still happily wandering in slumber-land when we came out to have our morning bath!"

Their mystery-solving dialogue was suddenly interrupted by a loud round of applause coming from the swarm of insects; they had been conducting their own investigation and had come to a conclusion already:

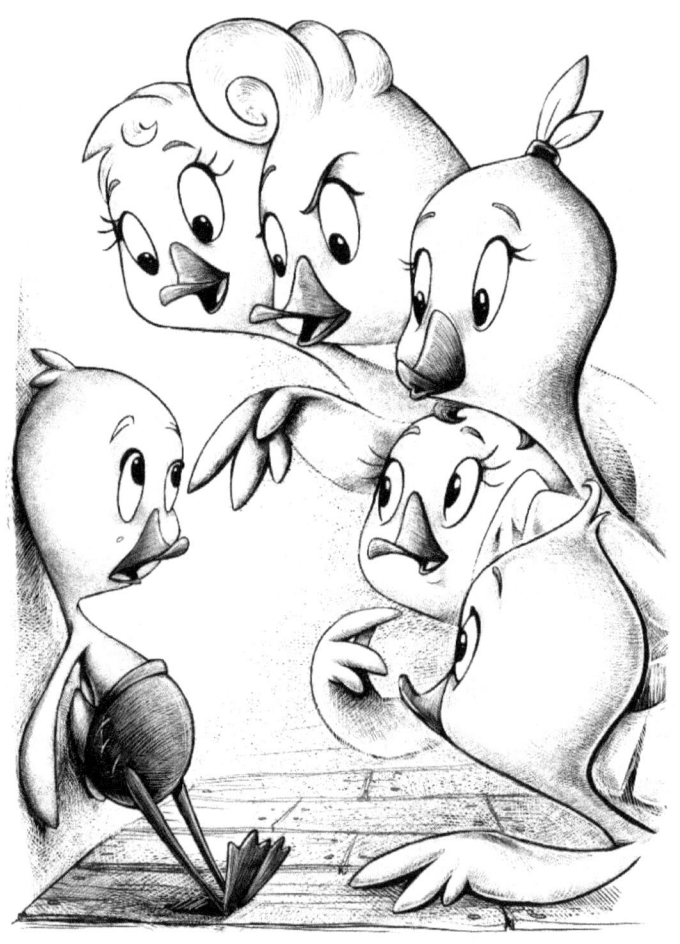

"Well done, young duckling, very well done!" they saluted Rica, before turning to his sisters to explain:

"This beauty spot is a special gift which your brother proved himself worthy of!"

"Who gave it to him, and perhaps even more importantly, what for?" one sister demanded clarification.

"The swallows gave it to him…"

"When did that happen?" the girls continued their questioning.

The elders of the insects stood up to get a better view and keep themselves awake as they followed the development of the story.

"Your little brother is the only one who can answer that question," one of the elders stated solemnly.

"Yeah, you tell them, Grandpa!" a youngster cheered from the middle of the swarm, casting admiring glances at Rica. The whole swarm turned around gliding on the spot, curious to see if the praise for Rica would be in any way acknowledged by his sisters. But they seem to be more interested in collateral details.

"It was a gift which you proved worthy for? What did you do to get it?" they asked looking at one another and thronging around Rica for answers. Rica couldn't help casting an irritated glance towards the young insect who so indiscreetly put out there details of his adventure from the previous day. The young insect covered his mouth apologetically, but it was too late: the word about Rica's beauty spot had already spread like wildfire and there was no way of stopping it.

Even Rica's sisters had been left with no doubts about the truth of that sensational revelation: Rica's gift was very special, indeed, and it had been granted by the swallows! But there were a lot more questions to answer. The oldest sister went over to the indiscreet insect to demand details, while the rest of them crowded around Rica, each raising her voice as they tried to make themselves heard in the racket and get an explanation from him. Even though he had been caught in the middle of the chaos, Rica managed to beckon the insect and plead for discretion: they needed to keep a lid over it! Then he looked up to see the position of the sun in the sky; time was going fast and he didn't have long until his playdate! Still, he realized he would never get out of there if he didn't satisfy his sisters curiosity! So, he cleared his throat and projected his voice:

"Everybody, stop right now!"

Silence fell over the place. Rica took everybody by surprise.

"If you promise me that you won't say anything to anyone, even to Mom and Dad, I'll tell you everything you want to know!" he vowed.

The sisters blinked quickly, looked one another in the eye, and one of them nodded to the others with a wink: they would agree to all his demands until they had found out all they wanted to know from him!

"Of course, of course, we promise!" the sisters sworn themselves to secrecy.

"Very well, then follow me!" he said, as he discreetly thanked the insects for their cooperation. Making out to his sisters that the insects would be excluded from this special moment of revealing confession, Rica headed to the house, opened the door, and disappeared inside, followed by his sisters who closed the door tightly behind them.

Playing along with Rica, the insects protested outraged:

"We want to know, as well! Tell us about it, please! It's not fair that we get left out of it! Is this the kind of thanks we are getting in return for our loyalty!" they insisted.

Eager to find out about the beauty spot, the ducklings ignored the choir of insects, as they shut the windows and pulled the curtains, barricading themselves in. A few lanky mosquitoes crept into a crack in the wall, trying to pry.

For the next half an hour Rica told them about his adventures from the previous day and how he got rewarded by the swallows. When Rica finished whispering his story, his sisters remained quiet for a while, until one of them asked:

"Where is the nest of the swallows?"

"What kind of question is that? Why do you want to know?" Rica was taken aback.

"It's just a question! We're testing you to see if you are telling the truth…" the oldest sister quipped.

"Don't you believe me?" Rica could hardly hide his disappointment at their suspicious attitude. But he remembered the talk he had with his dad and smiled inside: it would be a while until these ducklings changed!

"But of course we trust you!" the sisters rushed to correct him.

"Then what is it all about?" it was Rica's turn to ask.

"We just want to know the spot for ourselves!" they replied cautiously.

"OK, have it your way: the swallows nest near the lake down the road, the one funnily shaped like the hoof of a lamb!"

The ducklings stared at one another slightly confused.

"Girls, I expect better of you: can't you remember the story of the Aries, which stands for the sign of the ram in the zodiac? Legend has it that when it was a new born lamb, he was such a beautiful beast that the evil eye cast a curse on it out of jealousy, and the gods had to fetch him all the way here and had him graze some magic herbs which restored him back to health. They say the lake down the road from here is imprint of his hoof into the ground from time immemorial…"

The girls peeked at one another again, their memories of childhood stories kicked into touch by their little brother.

"Don't tell me you've forgotten about that magical night when gran and granddad showed us the star signs for the first time and told us the story of how each of them came into being!" Rica told them off.

"Oh, you mean that story…" the girls finally recalled that memorable night.

"Now that we are all on the same page, I can tell you that the swallows are nesting in the only willow tree there that binds water and ground together!" Rica told them, as he noticed with discontent a shadow of confusion descending in his sisters' eyes again. "There are many willow trees on the shore of the lake, but it's only one of them which enjoys the embrace of shallow waters and the sturdiness of the solid ground!" Rica clarified it for them.

If only they had the wisdom to read between the lines, that last detail revealed by their little brother would have saved them a lot of hassle if properly understood.

But Rica's sisters were but young ducklings far too busy chasing wild geese. As soon as they thought they knew everything they needed to know, they dropped

Rica like a hot potato and went off to talk matters amongst themselves. They all retreated in their bedroom closing the door behind them and leaving Rica to his own devices. After about ten minutes of intense arguing, the door burst open and they all thronged out in the living room and stopped in front of Rica who couldn't take his eyes off the reflection of his own face in the mirror. He still couldn't believe what he was seeing right there on his right cheek.

"We've decided to go to the lake ourselves!" they announced.

"I beg your pardon?" Rica's eyes bulged out of their sockets.

"We'd like to see it with our own eyes!" they informed Rica without batting an eyelash. "And you'll have to stay home until we come back!"

"Why?" Rica didn't like the sound of it.

"You'll have to stay here and keep an eye on the house for us. But don't get all gloomy about it, because this comes with some nice perks: you'll be able to entertain our fans and thus, share our popularity and the adoration of our followers!" they said proudly, while Rica was rolling his eyes. "Besides, you've had your reward from the swallows, and now it's our turn!" they let on the real reason of their journey to the lake.

One of the sisters quacked out:

"Leaving you in charge of the household and of our fans is a great honor! Enjoy it, but don't get too comfortable; we'll be back home before you could say duck, duck, goose!"

Another one nudged her to guard her tongue. It was not the time for playing smart.

"Mom and Dad said you shouldn't leave the household on your own!" Rica warned them as his mind played back at him the tragic story of Cockerel's family.

One of the mosquitoes hiding in the crack of the wall escaped in the room and buzzed noisily:

"Very well-remembered, lad! Children should listen to their parents and not go out on their own! Stranger danger!"

The girls turned around and if a stare could kill, the poor mosquito would have dropped dead then and there. Luckily, the mosquito found the crack in the wall straight away and flew out to tell the others the latest news.

Back in the living room, the sisters turned their attention to Rica.

"You are a fine one to talk, aren't you? Whose permission did you ask yesterday when you went off on your own?"

Rica kept silent.

"Yes, that's right," another one intervened, "You wandered off on your own, made some nice friends, got yourself a great gift from the swallows... What makes you think that we wouldn't be able to get out there and do as well for ourselves?"

"Ha, ha, ha!" they all burst into laughter at the thought that their little brother could even think of challenging them like that.

Rica wanted to object: he had a playdate to go to! But before he could say anything, his sisters had already reached the gate, slammed it open and off on their way to the lake they were! Rica watched them go accompanied by a cloud of young insects while the elder insects stayed behind and were on the verge of dozing off.

"I've got to tell you that you look really handsome with that beauty spot on your right cheek! If it's not a secret, do you mind telling us how you got it?" one of the more alert elders asked him politely.

Rica hesitated, which endeared him even more with the elders; his modesty stood him in good credit! Rica thought for a while; the elders were quite innocuous and wise enough to show discretion, so Rica decided to tell the tale. Far from falling asleep on him, the elder insects propped themselves up as well as they could and kept listening. At last, somebody was taking them into account and treating them with due respect; Rica's presence was a very welcome change and his story was enthralling and exciting! Time was flowing by like a snake tamed by the mesmerizing tune of a magic flute!

As opposed to the peaceful scene at home, the crowd of ducklings made their way to the lake in a hullaballoo. They soon arrived to the spot indicated by Rica and ordered the swarm of insects that had joining them to fly up and gather information from the nest. The insects did as asked, and they soon came back letting them know that the swallow parents were away.

"We couldn't have wished for a better time!" the oldest duckling smiled.

They all huddled together in a yellow circle of fluff, putting their heads together to hatch a plan. The sun made their fluff shimmer and shine, while the wind ruffled through it. But the ducklings had no time to waste; they were on a mission! Once a plan of action was agreed upon by everybody, they stood up and waddled into the water giggling and frolicking.

It wasn't long before their play in the water attracted the swallow chicks to the brim of their nest. The chicks were hanging above the edge watching the newcomers having fun in the water.

"Look at these ducklings! They look like the one from yesterday, except these ones are all girls!" the swallow chicks talked amongst themselves.

When the ducklings saw them hanging over the edge watching down, they stopped for a moment and acted surprised:

"Look up, girls! We've got company!" they spoke out loud so that the chicks could hear them.

Then they kept swimming and splashing for a while until the oldest cleared her voice and addressed her sisters loud enough to be heard from the nest:

"Aren't those chicks the cutest things under the sun?" she exclaimed.

Having drawn their attention already, the oldest duckling called out to the swallow chicks:

"Hello there! Do you fancy getting down here for a splash and a splosh?"

A few of the youngest chicks climbed on the brim of the nest unthinkingly, ready to let themselves fall in the water underneath, but the older ones intervened just in the nick of time to stop them and give them a good telling off.

"Haven't you learnt anything from what happened to our brother yesterday?" they scolded.

The young chicks stopped in their tracks and climbed back down in the nest, peaking at a window through which their adventurous brother was watching everything from inside. He had been grounded to stay inside while his parents were away from the nest, and judging by the frightened look in his eyes, he had no wish to be outside for the time being.

Although aware of the danger, the little chicks were still longing to take part in the ducklings' games and fun. One of the older chicks put his head out of the nest and called down to the ducklings:

"We wish we could join in, but our wings are not ready for flight yet!" and he flapped his frail wings to support his words.

But the ducklings didn't seem convinced:

"What's flight got to do with it? If you come down we can carry you on our backs and play battleships, we can ferry you up and down the lake and we'll have *great fun together!" they insisted bobbing up and down on the water, swimming on the spot and splashing water at one another by twerking their tails.*

"Come on in, you can trust us!" they continued to tempt the baby swallows.

"Sorry, but we are not getting anywhere near the water! It's out of the question!" the older swallow chicks replied firmly. "In fact, I advise you to be cautious because a fierce pike prowls around here beneath the surface of the water!" the wise chick continued. "Admittedly, he hasn't got as many sharp teeth as he used to, but I suspect he is not alone!"

Too hyped up and overexcited at the thought of getting their own beauty spots, the ducklings chose to ignore the baby swallow's warning. They came together again for a change of plans, as their scheming so far wasn't going their way. After a short council, one of the ducklings spoke to the baby swallows again:

"You are right about the dangers of playing in the water, maybe that wasn't such a good idea! But why don't we get to know each other better by telling stories? We've got a story to share with you and we think you would enjoy it very much. Why don't you just shuffle down on the lower branches of the willow tree, so you are closer to us and hear better?"

The baby swallows, especially the younger ones, saw no problem with the suggestion of the ducklings. The got themselves all worked up in anticipation of the wonderful story promised by the ducklings. The older chicks opposed again, but this time to no avail. The swallow chicks were now divided into two parties, and the ones eager to hear the story had already started their way down on the branches of the willow tree.

That was the opportunity which the ducklings had been hoping for all along. The oldest, being the strongest, stretched her neck and grasped the tip of a low branch in her beak, and started shaking it back and forth. That was enough for the baby swallows to lose their balance and fall through the branches of the willow. But the ducklings were ready for this moment, and luckily, each baby swallow landed in the arms of a duckling. Scared and confused, the swallows were shouting and screaming, terrified. The noise attracted Pike to the spot.

"Thank goodness for the opportunity to revenge my crumpled style!" he sneered as he shot through the water and had a good go at the ducklings, clipping their tails as they all rushed out to the shore warned by the panicked swarm of insects... When Pike finished the job, an awful lot of yellow fluff was floating on the waters of the lake, as the ducklings were sorrowfully checking their rear ends! As soon as they

were back on dry land, the ducklings put the baby swallows down safely. They were soggy, scared, and upset.

The only ones left laughing were the insects! Now that the danger was over, the sight of the sorry tailless ducklings made them roar with laughter! These little madams finally got what they deserved!

"You might want to come and get your yellow scum back!" Pike dared them from the middle of the lake, angry at himself to have missed another opportunity for a hearty meal.

Eventually, the Mother and Father Swallow arrived back to the nest. The last thing they expected was the sight of half of their babies wet and distressed mingling with a bunch of ducklings at the bottom of the willow tree. The wiser half of their children who had enough sense to stay in the nest were watching helpless and guiltily from above. Mother Swallow wanted to say something, but her husband put a wing around her shoulders and stopped her. It was wise to find out what happened first! Pike sank in the water, not daring to challenge anything bigger than a chick!

"I'll be with you shortly!" Mother Swallow promised the ducklings as she and Father Swallow took their babies up to the nest. While wiping dry the scared chicks, Mother and Father Swallow had time to listen to their children' account of what had happened: a bunch of ducklings showed up out of the blue and started frolicking in the water, tempting the chicks in. Eventually, they lured some of the chicks on the lower branches of the willow by promising them a wonderful story.

Mother and Father Swallow said nothing but looked at each other knowingly. They understood in an instant what motivated the ducklings. After briefly assessing the situation, Mother Swallow decided what reward the ducklings deserved; and it needed to come with a lesson which they would never forget, as well! Carried away by their own desires, the ducklings not only put themselves in danger, but they recklessly put the chicks in the way of harm! Still, Mother Swallow didn't forget for one moment that they were young children, silly and naïve, more than anything else!

"You can stay here and look after the children, and I'll go down to the ducklings!" Mother Swallow instructed Father Swallow while peeking over the edge of the nest at the ducklings who were either waving up at her putting their chopped up tails up in the air to point out their loss worth rewarding, or keeping their heads down in shame and trying to hide away their pitiful behinds.

Mother Swallow went into the nest and picked up a golden box with a kind smile on her face. She flew down where she spoke first:

"Very many thanks for your bravery, my dear ducklings!"

"Oh, don't even mention it! Can you imagine, we were just passing by when we heard a terrible noise and desperate cries for help! It was just sheer luck that we happened to be nearby, otherwise the poor babies could have drowned!" the ducklings said dramatically.

They were so busy building themselves up in front of Mother Swallow, that none of them noticed the smile hanging in the corner of her beak; she knew the whole truth from her children, but didn't have the heart to put the young ducklings to shame.

"Well, thank you very much for that, girls, and sorry for your tails!" Mother Swallow subtly made her point.

"That's quite all right, we are just happy that we could help, otherwise a tragedy might have happened! You can tell how nasty Pike is by our poor tails... or what's left of them, anyway!" the ducklings fell for it.

"You've got to look at the positives: it's only fluff, it will grow back!" Mother Swallow stifled a giggle.

"That'll take a while... Such a shame about our beautiful tails!" one of them felt terribly sorry for herself.

Inspired by her comments, a younger sister who was standing next to Mother Swallow mustered all her courage and stuck her tongue out at Pike. The fish went dark with spite and ground his teeth. The frightening noise which came out of his jaws made everybody's hair stand on end. But there is a price to pay for everything and Pike was to find that out a few seconds later when he had to spit out another one of his teeth ... Aggrieved and defeated, Pike disappeared in the depth of the lake, while a few cheeky mosquitoes loitering around were laughing their heads off at his misfortune.

Mother Swallow shook her head wisely:

"There is a rightful payment for every deed, good and bad! Speaking of which, my dear ducklings, I'm thinking of rewarding you for what you've done today!"

"Yuppy! Beauty spots!" one of the ducklings let her mouth run with it.

"You, silly, little girl, don't give us away!" another one nudged her.

But Mother Swallow heard her. It confirmed her suspicions: the striking resemblance between Rica and his sisters did not go unnoticed with Mother Swallow. As for the rest, she filled in the blanks rather easily: the little drake from the day before must have had all his siblings on his case, once they saw his beauty spot. Like all children, these lasses wanted some beauty spots for themselves, and therefore the idea of a pretend rescue which was supposed to bring them the much-wanted reward!

"Beauty spots you say... But of course!" she whispered knowingly.

The ducklings were jumping out of their skins with joy: for them it was mission accomplished!

"We'll make you proud, and that's a promise!" one of the girls chortled excitedly. "And when you think that everybody in the land will find out about us..." she carried on.

"Since you've put your own lives in danger to save other innocent lives, you are well deserving of widespread fame!" Mother Swallow played along, trying hard to keep a straight face. She looked up at her babies who were watching everything from above. In readiness to receive their reward, the ducklings wasted no time: they lined up in order of height, shortest to tallest, right in front of Mother Swallow. When she turned her attention to them again, she could hardly stifle a chuckle.

Seeing them so eager, she took out the golden box and opened it. The ducklings had to shade their eyes from the blinding light flooding out of it. With all the excitement, they never noticed that their reward was coming from a golden box, rather than a red one, like their brother mentioned!

Mother Swallow gently placed a golden drop on the cheek of each of them. The ducklings quacked loudly, admiring each other. After only a few minutes, a cheekier one went to Mother Swallow and pleaded:

"Don't they look just wonderful on us? Since the beauty spots suit us so well, do you think we could get another one each? Everybody knows how generous you are; word of it has been travelling right around the land!"

"More than one for each of you?" Mother Swallow lowered her voice as if in warning, thinking to herself that the likelihood between Rica and his sisters went no further than their appearance; the girls' selfish attitude blatantly stood out when measured up against Rica's modesty.

"Yes, yes, more beauty spots for each of us!" they chanted.

"So be it!" Mother Swallow agreed. "Just bear with me!" she said as she twitched her nose a few times, and let out a lady-like sneeze. Although she shielded her beak with a wing, she made sure that the airflow traveled all the way to the girls and stroked their young cheeks. The ducklings were oblivious at Mother Swallow's subtle maneuver, and giggled to themselves calling out:

"Bless you!"

"And you!" Mother Swallow answered quickly with a smile.

From where she stood, Mother Swallow could see that her plan worked: the warm breath carried by the power of the pretend sneeze splattered the golden drops into tens of droplets all over their faces.

"That's it, girls, you've had your wish. Just remember that your spots will really become yours with the first hug or kiss from somebody who truly loves you. You deserve this reward more than anyone else. Be safe as you travel back home and look after yourselves!" Mother Swallow told the girls as she prepared to return to the nest.

Baffled, the ducklings stared at her not knowing what to make of it; they expected Mother Swallow to resort to her supply in the golden box. Instead, Mother Swallow closed the tiny box with a dramatic flick of the wing.

"Have faith, girls!" she called out to them, but the ducklings shuffled from one leg to another in a huff.

"You're welcome, anyway, and have a safe journey home!" Mother Swallow put them on the spot for forgetting their manners.

"Just one more thing, if I may!" one of the ducklings quacked from the crowd.

"Please feel free to ask, my child!" Mother Swallow stopped in her tracks.

"When can we expect to become famous all over the land?" the same duckling asked without batting an eyelash.

"You mean become famous for our good deed today," another one squared things up for everybody to understand. "The kind of adventure that we had today is well worth the fame and fortune which comes with it! We've had our fortune," she continued pointing at her own cheek, "and hopefully, the fame is not far behind..."

"The fame, of course, of course..." Mother Swallow nodded her head as she made efforts not to burst into laughter. "You'll be famous all over the land no later than tomorrow! Everybody will find out about it!" Mother Swallow solemnly promised, then muttered to herself amused:

"Some adventure that comes with fame and fortune...."

"Is that a promise?!" the ducklings insisted.

"You have my word, girls! You won't be able to get away from fame, even if you wanted to!" Mother Swallow predicted.

"Hurray!" the unsuspecting ducklings cheered loudly.

One of the insects in the swarm which was hovering over, raised her voice over the background buzzing:

"Hey, what about us? We did our bit in warning the ducklings about Pike..."

"Zip it, sister!" Another insect told her off. "We'll get something out of it at some point in the future, now that we know where to come for an adventure with rewards!" she said winking.

"Thank you a thousand times!" the ducklings waddled happily this way and that way, unable to contain their excitement.

"The pleasure is all mine!" Mother Swallow assured them.

Waving goodbye and rather elated about the outcome of their adventure, the ducklings set out for home. As they pushed open the gate, their little brother welcomed them asking details about their enterprise. But his sisters marched past him, ignoring him completely as they exchanged impressions amongst themselves. One of the insects who witnessed his sisters' quest for fame and fortune flew down and sat himself on Rica's shoulder to tell him the whole story from the beginning to the end. Rica sighed heavily; his sisters never learnt... The sight of their ragged tails, however, put a smile on his face: he felt somewhat vindicated! As soon as they arrived home, the ducklings went in front of their apathetic audience, the elderly insects, and started boasting about their beauty spots and the good name they had earned for themselves by dint of their valor! They even told everybody how Mother Swallow agreed to present them with a bunch of beauty spots each as a token of her appreciation. Eager to prove themselves right, they took out their pocket mirrors and eyeliners and began dotting beauty spots all over their faces... and the racket they made in the process was enough to deafen anyone...

Rica decided to leave them to their own devices. He opened the gate and let himself out like the previous day, and like the previous day none of his sisters noticed him go. Only a few insects worried about his well-being followed him closely.

Rica walked fast trying to make up for his delayed departure, but before long he could see a throng of birds coming from the opposite direction. The eagle-eyed duckling could spot his parents in the crowd and he straight away turned back on himself, got home in no time and took himself inside pretending to be engrossed in a make-believe game as if nothing happened.

When the parents set foot in the front garden, the girls welcomed them as usual. Their mom kissed each of their foreheads and took a good look at their tails:

"What have you been up to, girls?" she wanted to know.

The ducklings lowered their stare ashamed and the oldest explained:

"We got rid of some fluff here and there, just to keep ourselves cool! You know how much we like experimenting with fashion…" she said convincingly. Mother Duck frowned at them, then cast a glance at Father Duck who shrugged his shoulders amused. The ducklings understood their father's light-hearted take on things would allow them to get away with it, so they all rushed ahead cuddling into him making a great fuss.

"What have you done to your faces?" Father Duck asked noticing the eyeliner smudges.

"It's nothing, we've put on some make-up! Today we had fun trying new ideas in our fashion show." the girls swiftly brushed off the comment.

Mother and Father Duck smiled and said nothing. They all went inside, washed and had dinner together as usual. The girls were restless, and at bedtime they eagerly reminded Mother Duck about their promise to cuddle them to sleep that night. Mother Duck hadn't forgotten: she kissed each of them on the forehead before they settled for the night.

Early in the morning next day, the parents set out for the market place, leaving their children fast asleep in their beds. The first one to wake up was one of the girls whose bed was close to the window; a playful ray of sun had sneaked in and was swinging on her eyelashes warding off all the sweet morning dreams. The duckling opened her eyes grumpily for being woken up so early on, only to remember what a big day it was:

"Beauty spots, here we come!" she whispered with eager anticipation.

Her first impulse was to wake up everybody else, but changed her mind on second thought. She nimbly jumped out of bed and ran in front of the mirror where some random sunrays played hide-and-seek. With one quick look in the mirror, her world was rocked to the core; she anxiously rubbed her face all over, but whatever she was trying to get rid of, was obviously still there. She gave a sharp shriek and her knees gave up on her! She felt numb in her body and a suspicion nudged at the edges of her mind: Mother Swallow had seen right through their deception and her reward was a perfect match of their deed! Under the shock of that revelation, the duckling screamed again and again. One by one, all her sisters got out of bed, looking confused and scared: they couldn't understand what had brought their sister into such a state of despair! But one quick glimpse in the mirror left them in no doubt about the cause of their sister's distress:

"Oh, no, this is a disaster!" they wailed.

They rushed over to Rica's bed to wake him up.

"What's gotten into you this morning, you crazy girls!" he told them off half asleep. But when he opened his eyes and saw what a sight his sisters were, he sat up and reached out to touch their faces. He wiped gently, but nothing was coming off. He wiped harder, but still no good! When he finally understood what happened, he burst into uncontrollable laughter…"

"But why was Rica so amused?" I asked, unable to control my own curiosity. "What could he see on their faces?"

Mother smiled and explained:

"Instead of one stylish beauty spot adorning their cute faces, they had a multitude of freckles; when Mother Swallow sneezed in their direction, her warm breath managed to pulverize the golden drop into tens of tiny droplets which were now covering their faces and necks!"

"Did Mother Swallow do that?" I asked, taken aback by the turn in the story.

"She did, indeed! Swallows are kind and generous, but they are nobody's fools: they give each what they deserve!" Mom added.

"Wasn't that a bit harsh?" I asked still shocked.

"Not at all, if you think about it, that was a mild punishment: the ducklings went to the swallows' house and put their children in danger for a very frivolous reason, which was nothing short of reckless!" Mom cleared it for me.

My sisters, who had been following the story with wide open eyes and barely breathing, stared at each other and put their hands out to touch their faces; they had freckles very much like the ducklings in the story. While they were still quietly ruminating on the meaning of the story, Mom and I were laughing our heads off at the funny twist in the tale. We laughed so much that, in the end, even my siblings who had fallen asleep woke up asking what was going on.

"What happened after that?" I question Mom when we calmed down a bit.

The speckled ducklings blamed their misfortune on their brother. Thy even hatched a plot to go back and take revenge for what Mother Swallow had done to them, but a wise old insect advised them to abandon such thought if they didn't want to get pimples on their tongues!

In the end, the ducklings resigned themselves to having to put up with the freckles, knowing fully well that they had brought it on themselves.

Mother Swallow, however, kept her promise through and through: before the next day at dawn, everybody had found out the true story of the sly ducklings who tried to get an undeserved reward using lies and deception. Thus, the ducklings' wish of being known all over the land had come true, but not quite in the way they wanted it; famous can, through a funny twist of fate, easily turn to infamous! As for their freckles, they were there to stay and remind them of the importance of being honest, and kind and truthful.

When the parents came home, the ducklings didn't dare come out in daylight for fear that they would be laughed at. After a moment's panic at the unusual peace and quiet of the household, Mother and Father Duck discovered their offspring in the house, not knowing what to make of their new look. As soon as they caught sight of them, the parents had an almighty fit of laughter, much to their daughters' discontent. But seeing the girls so unhappy didn't sit right with them.

"You can't get that upset only because of some freckles! If anything, they bring up your beautiful eyes and make your wonderful smile stand out!" they encouraged the girls

"Do you really think so?" the girls brightened up instantly.

"Freckles definitely suit you! In fact, I wanted to let you into a secret... I was saving it for when you were a bit older, but now that this happened, I think you might be happy to find out about it!" Mother Duck appeased them as she turned to each of them for a cuddle and a kiss. Mother Duck's affection worked wonders and the ducklings quietened down ready to hear the secret their mom wanted to share with them. Mom gently guided them into the living room where they all settled down. The flickering candle light swayed this way and that way, letting Mother Duck know that a terrible hullaballoo had been going on just minutes before her arrival. Mother

Duck bowed her head as she took everything in, then she addressed her daughters in a whispering voice:

"You should know, my dear girls, that all the good men of royal blood..." she intentionally paused and looked around to make sure she had their full attention. The ducklings were listening to her with their necks stretched, hardly breathing.

"... who live in lavish palaces on remote exotic islands..." and she waited for a few seconds before she delivered the big news: "... well, those princes only want to marry girls with freckles, like you!" she finally broke it to them.

"Isn't this lucky?" the ducklings jumped up and down flapping their wings with glee.

"Very lucky, indeed!" their mom confirmed with a smile.

That was enough for the ducklings to get their mojo back: they all rushed to get as good as possible a spot in front of the mirror where they could count their freckles in a competition to see which one was the most desirable. They were rapt dreaming about their prince on a white horse, and the happiness on their faces spoke for itself."

"May The Almighty bless all parents with good wits when they talk their children out of their silly ideas!" Mom rounded up the story.

"When she went back outside, Mother Duck had a little chat with the insects who told her all about the encounters of Mother Swallow and her children. Fully in the know, Mother Duck pondered a while over the events and could find no flaw with the way Mother Swallow dealt with Rica and his sisters. All she had to do now was apply herself with wisdom and patience and help her children make the most of their luck.

She went over to Rica, who was on his own inside, sat him on her knees and told him in a tender voice:

"I am very proud of you, my little ball of fluff! Word about your bravery and good judgment has reached far and wide in the land and I just wanted to tell you that I couldn't wish for a better son!"

Rica hugged his mom, resting his head close to her heart for a while. She was happy now knowing what she knew, and that was the best feeling in the world for him!"

"And this is where the story ends..." Mom announced looking around at us all.

"What about Rica and his friends? Have they met again?" I asked unwilling to let her go.

"What do you think?" she replied.

"I want them to stay friends forever!" I told her, secretly wishing the same kind of friends for myself.

"That is a very nice thought and you should keep to it! The story ends the way you want it to end!" Mom encouraged me to dare to dream. She stood up and kissed my beauty spot.

"Nighty-night, my little ducklings!" she said.

I firmly caught her hand as she was passing by.

"What now?" she turned to me.

"What did Magpie have against Cuckoo?" I steered her back into the story.

"Well, Magpie in the story must have brought up Cuckoo's chick which the latter had abandoned. Later on, when that chick became a grown-up in his own right, Cuckoo tried winning him back by bribing Magpie with a measly worm which he didn't even bother catching, but rather got hold of by cheating and lying."

"But what's wrong in wanting to get back your own children?" I still couldn't get my head around Magpie's grudge against Cuckoo.

"It's nothing wrong in that, but Cuckoo should have thought twice before remorselessly abandoning his own offspring in somebody else's nest!" Mom explained.

"What do you mean remorselessly? It's not what Cuckoo said to Rica!" I protested.

"You are right, it's not, so I guess Cuckoo was spinning him a yarn, trying to impress him and get what he wanted out of him!" Mom whispered.

"What did he want from the duckling?" I felt my head starting to spin around.

"Cuckoo hoped to get information that would lead him to the worm with a star on his forehead! Anyway, to make a long story short, Magpie had taken on Cuckoo's chick and raised him as her own, which is not an easy thing to do. Magpie gave him a good education, spent time with the chick and taught him everything she knew, only to have the selfish Cuckoo showing up at the end to get his chick back. Magpie, like any mother in this world, wouldn't take that lying!" Mom added trying to free her hand from my grasp and go off.

"But why did Cuckoo abandoned his egg in another nest?" I wouldn't give up on my questions.

Mom peeked at me from the side, thinking for a few seconds how she could best make me understand such a complicated thing:

"Cuckoos are selfish and ignorant birds, they carelessly abandon their offspring in other nests and go off on their way. But in time, they get to experience regret and a longing for their long lost children, so they go back for them trying to win them over. This is a primordial call in all of us and from a certain age, the cuckoo wants to make sure that his offspring will carry on!"

"But why?"

"It's their way of easing off the feeling of guilt which burdens them greatly after a while!"

I listened to Mom mesmerized. I liked to listen to the cuckoo's song during summer nights, but its way of life and the stories surrounding it were completely alien to me.

"That's it, no more talk! It's time you went to sleep! It's late now!"

I grasped her hand again:

"Why is the cuckoo so bad at parenting its own children? Is it a curse or something? I can't think of many things worse than not being able to bring up your own children!" I said, determined to find out more.

"There is a legend which explains why the cuckoo is the way he is, but I'll tell it to you when you are a bit older!" Mom stroked my head.

"Why not tell it to me now?" I insisted.

"You are far too young for a story like that and you won't understand. Besides, there are things in this story which are better left for later on. I don't want you growing up too soon, Gheorghita!" Mom explained.

"Please, Mom!" I pleaded.

"Enough talk for tonight! I'll tell you more about it tomorrow! Good night, sleep tight!" Mom bent over and kissed me on the head.

I let her hand go as I knew she had to wake up early in the morning and go to work, but I continued whispering as I was touching my beauty spot:

"Who gave me this beauty spot, Mom!"

"It must have been a swallow, of course!" Mom laughed quietly.

"You reckon?" I sat up in bed excitedly. "What did I do to earn it? "

"I'm afraid I don't know anything about that, but I'm sure one day you'll remember and tell me all about it, as well!"

"When did I encounter the swallow?" I wanted to know.

"The only one who can answer that question is you. But I should imagine that you were very little at the time of the encounter, that's why you can't remember it. I'm sure, though that you've done some great acts of bravery to deserve it. Don't worry, one day it will all come back to you. Life is full of surprises, and we have to be ready to take up on all opportunities which come our way. Everything in its own time, little man!" Mom said and kissed me on the head again.

She stood up and went off to bed. I remember being unable to go to sleep for a long time that night. I watched the ghostly shadows of the trees outside morphing into mystical creatures I had never seen or heard of before. I felt my beauty spot in the dark and a sense of unexplained pride filled me to the brim. Besides, the oddity of the cuckoo story had left me baffled. I used to enjoy listening to the cuckoo's trills during the long summer days, but I knew nothing of its strange behavior; that night I decided in my mind to give the cuckoo the benefit of the doubt: the bird must have had a good reason for displaying such bad parenting skills!

When I finally fell asleep, all I dreamt about was the magic of the beauty spot, which was to follow me in the years to come, as it became a symbol of my identity.

It wasn't long before Maria, shrewd cookie as she was, worked out how much the beauty spot meant to me; every time she wanted me sworn to secrecy, she would make me vow on my beauty spot not to disclose the 'big secrets' that she revealed to me. I have to confess, however, that Maria's success in doing that relied on my long-held belief that one day I would find out the special reason which had qualified me for such a special gift. Despite growing up at a fast pace during those years, it was never a doubt in my mind that my mom had told me the truth about my beauty spot and her prediction stuck in my memory to this day. In fact, it is often the reason for merry-meaning and laughter in the family gatherings from today. Maria, especially, always has a funny story to tell about my beauty spot and the way she used to tease me about it when we were children.

Whenever we didn't see eye-to-eye, she would pretend to pluck off my beauty spot, put it on her tongue, and eat it!

"That's it, all gone!" she would wind me up even more. "That's what happens to naughty little boys who don't listen to their big sisters: they lose their favorite beauty spot!"

Needless to say, that I believed her every time, and her words together with her boisterous manner were enough to send me around the twist: I would wail and cry my eyes out, running after her as I implored:

"Please, give it back, give it back!"

Not only did Maria enjoy seeing me in distress, but she was killing herself laughing as if my suffering was tickling her. Our poor mom would drop whatever she was doing at the time and came running to see what was going on.

"If I had to make one wish that would be to see the day when you two will get along fine with each other!" she would tell us off in her own way.

As soon as I saw her, I would run to her and tell her everything about my ordeal. My mom would smile understandingly, take my head in her hands, and give me a kiss on the cheek, right in the place of my beauty spot.

"Here you are, Gheorghita! Your beauty spot is back on!" she reassured me.

But my scare was such, that I wouldn't even believe her until she showed me in the mirror. Happy and relieved, I would rush to give her a cuddle while sticking my tongue out at my sister behind Mom's back.

Seeing that my sister's pranks carried on without fail and there was no sign she would stop soon, one day Mom took me aside and told me:

"Listen up, Gheorghita: when Maria tells you that she's taken your beauty spot, instead of getting upset, you should run to the mirror and check to see if your beauty spot is still in place. If it's not there, come quickly to me and we'll have it back in its place in no time with a kiss on the cheek! Just like that!" Mom winked at me.

The look in my eyes must have given away the doubt in my heart because Mom felt the need to remind me:

"You haven't forgotten about the words of Mother Swallow, have you? A kiss of genuine love will make the beauty spot show up in plain sight!"

Mom's words would cheer me up and put a smile on my face again, until the next time when Maria would come up with something else to drive me on the brink of desperation. Having worked out that I wasn't that easily impressed by her pranks, she started hiding the mirrors from me and even locked me out of the house so that I couldn't see myself in the big wall mirror.

"Don't even think of jumping in through the window, because a big, bad wolf is waiting inside and he'll have you for dinner in no time!" she would threaten me.

The thought of a fierce, famished beast lurking in the shadows terrified me, and I would run to Mom to tell her everything about it.

"What's the matter, my darling?" Mom would ask.

"My beauty spot!"

"Not again! Have you looked for it in the mirror?"

"I can't find any mirrors; Maria hid them all from me!" I complained.

"You've got to improvise: have a glance in a well-polished window, or in a water puddle. Make it up as you go along, dear boy, and don't let her have her way!" Mom taught me.

One year on my birthday Mom gave me a little pocket mirror. Only the two of us were supposed to know about it and for a long time I managed to keep it away from Maria's eyes. Thus, every time she teased me about my beauty spot, I ran and hide and looked in my mirror

But as I gained in confidence thinking that Maria's teasing had already come to an end, my sister grew frustrated for not being able to succeed in pranking me like she used to. In the end, it turned out that she managed to get her hands on my pocket mirror and as soon as that happened, she was back at her old tricks. I remember a sunny summer day when I upset her, and, as usual. She pretended to steal my beauty spot. Our cat was dozing off on the porch making easy prey for Maria who grabbed her and pretended to stick my beauty spot underneath her tail. Having had such a rude awakening, the cat plunged into a frenzy and started struggling to get away.

"Scram!" Maria eventually put her down and scared her away, hoping the cat would run as far as possible before I managed to catch it.

Panicked that my beauty spot could be forever lost if the cat got away, I rushed after her in tears. As soon as I caught her in the middle of the courtyard, desperately seeking my beauty spot under her tail. Mom, who was doing some chores around, saw us. The meowing cat and I must have made a sorry sight to look at, and Mom asked:

"Gheorghita, what on earth are you doing to that cat?"

"I'm looking for my beauty spot under her tail! Maria put it there!" I answered promptly.

Mom stared at us in disbelief: my sister had really overstepped all boundaries this time! She walked to me, took me in her arms and kissed me on the cheek, then asked:

"Where is your pocket mirror?"

"Maria took it away from me," I explained seizing the opportunity to tell her about the wolf waiting to snatch me if I went in the house.

"Gheorghita, my boy, you must stop believing everything she tells you; the beauty spot is in its place, on your cheek, and there is no such thing as a big, bad wolf in our house! Go to the big mirror inside and see for yourself!" Mom encouraged me nodding her head disapprovingly at my sister's ways.

Mom gently freed the cat out of my hands, gave me a stroke on the head, and went inside. After only a few seconds, I saw Maria rushing out like a whirlwind. She only stopped to glance back when she was at a safe distance up the road. Mom must have given her a piece of her mind reinforcing it with some hard rod, since she was still holding the broom by the other end when she finally made an appearance. From that blessed day on, Maria didn't dare play her tricks on me… not as far as my beauty spot was concerned, anyway!

Still, now and again, Maria would still have me vow on my beauty spot when she wanted to make sure she could rely on my silence or loyalty. She knew how important my beauty spot was to me and how tightly it linked into my identity, and she never hesitated to take advantage of it as much as she could.

Many years later, following the advice of a well-reputed doctor from Holland, I chose to undergo small surgery in order to get rid of some pimples of an inconclusive nature which had appeared on my face out of the blue. The above-mentioned doctor tried persuading me to do away with my 'legendary' beauty spot, but I refused.

"It's nothing to worry about," he reassured me, "we've been doing this type of small surgery for many years and we've never experienced any problems…"

Since time was of no issue to us both on that occasion, I recounted him the story of that beauty spot.

"If you don't mind me asking, are you a writer?" he questioned me with a smile.

"Yes, I am a writer amongst other things!" I replied.

"In that case, congratulations on your great talent, and I must say that I agree with you on this one: I wouldn't get rid of my signature feature, either!" he commented approvingly.

But going back to my story, my relationship with Maria has changed in time. Her pranks carried on for a while, but in a slightly different shape and form. As we were growing up, our needs were growing with us. As a girl, Maria found that she needed more money to keep up with her peers.

As I have already mentioned at an earlier stage in the story, our only source of income as a family was the livestock trade. We would grow animals from babies and sell them off for a bit of money. Those animals were nothing short of family members, always well taken care of and well treated!

After each of these transactions, Mom would give us some money as a reward for the hard work we had put in to help bring up those animals. As children, we all had our own reserve. We were taught work ethic alongside the importance of saving money. Although I was pretty good at saving my money, I didn't quite understand their true value. We would have the silver coins, carrying more value than the golden ones. Taking advantage of my liking of golden coins, Maria would have me exchange my silver coins for her golden ones.

You can imagine my bafflement as a child when I would go to the shop and I would only get a couple of small sweets for a fistful of golden coins.

"These sweets are really expensive!" I would say to myself on the way home.

With sweets being such a dear commodity, I could hardly bring myself to eat them. I used to treasure them, much preferring to look at them than gobble them up. With such a lot of my money going on just a few sweets, I would see them as luxury expenditure and hold on to them for a long time.

But one day, my mom took me on her knees and asked me:

"Gheorghita, how much have you been saving after this season's trade?"

I hurried to fetch the little sock which served as my money box. I was too small to count yet!

"But, dear boy, where are all the silver coins which I've given you?" Mom exclaimed.

"I've given them all to Maria in exchange for golden ones… You know they are hardly worth anything, Mom!" I retorted confidently.

Mom shook her head as if bothered by a swarm of flies.

"Gheorghita, I'll tell you something: the golden coins are less valuable than the silver ones. From now on, you'll know!"

I realized that my sister had tricked me again, but a deal is a deal. She wouldn't have given any of it back, anyway! Besides, I was a man of my word, even when Maria took advantage of me! By the time I was ten, I knew the value of money, coins and notes, I could count them properly and nobody could fool me!

Maria would also trick me into disclosing to her the place where I hid my savings, under the pretext of having to move it around for airing, like you would do with hay stacks. Otherwise, she would say, money can catch mold! But that trick was only short lived, as I soon wised it up to it all!

I worked by the season and made sure I raked in as much money as I could: whether it was trick or treating, or selling fruit and vegetables which I used to clandestinely harvest from the communal fields of the coop, it all added up in the end.

Thus, picking up one lucrative job after another, my stash grew to a considerable amount. When Mom took me with her to the nearest town, I would buy clothes for myself out of my own money.

With six strong and healthy children growing up, the income in the family increased as we were able to harvest almost as much as Mom. Dad had a fixed wage, but Mom was paid according to the amount of crop she could harvest.

When Mom was paid, she would get stacks of banknotes thoroughly packed up: each stack would have a certain number of banknotes tightly held together by two security strips running across each other and stamped at the ends. It was a precautionary method that ensured all workers were paid fairly, since not everybody was literate in basic numeracy. People would take to the bank the sealed banknote stacks to put away as rainy-day savings, and kept behind the loose cash to use it for small expenditures around the house.

People were very savvy with their money in those days: they would save for their old age and for important events like weddings and funerals. Some of them were simply afraid to keep a lot of money in the house!

My mom belonged to both those categories. With four girls to get married at some point, Mom was building up the dowry stash like a busy bee! During the summer and autumn months her earnings were substantially more than Dad's fixed salary: she would bring in 400 rubles a month on average, compared to Dad who was only earning 120 rubles a month.

Mom would have the 100, 300, and 500-ruble notes given to her in stacks and anything beyond that would be handed over to her in loose cash. Mom always took me with her when she went to the bank to safely place the money in the account. She jokingly called me her bodyguard, since there was no such thing as robbery or street violence in those days. It was a time of grace, very much like the reign of Vlad the Impaler during which theft and robbery had been eradicated by instilling notoriously harsh punishments for those in the wrong!

The cashier would take in the banknote stacks without counting the money as long as the security strips were in place. She put down in Mom's check book the amounts cashed in, and certify it by applying a small stamp.

After carefully watching the process a few times, an idea crossed my mind. In order to put it into practice, however, I needed to conduct some research of my own!

"What's bothering you, Gheorghita? You look like a cat on a hot roof!" Mom noticed I was a bit out of sorts.

"It's nothing, Mom, just a common cold!" I lied through my teeth and quickly went out for fear that I might give myself away.

I was itching to get hold of one of those banknote stacks, so the next time when Mom was paid, I went up to her and asked her for one. Mom handed it over to me without thinking twice about it; the thought of me tempering with her money stack never crossed her mind.

"Just make sure you don't disturb the security strips, son, because we are taking it to the bank, as usual!" she reminded me. "What is it that you want to see, anyway? How much it weighs?" she enquired with a smile.

I laughed, neither confirming nor denying Mom's suggestion.

"I only want to hold it for a little while!" Perfect timing, my dad and my sister entered the room

"That's an interesting thought…" Mom frowned slightly. "And why is that?"

"For good luck! They say it rubs off!" I chuckled.

"Good luck with what, Son?" Mom still couldn't understand.

"Good luck with everything! They say money gives you wings: if you've got it, you can fly, if you haven't, you'll have to crawl!" I explained my logic.

It was Mom's turn to laugh as she gave me the pack of money. In perfect timing, dad and my sister entered the room at that point, distracting Mom and giving me the chance to sit down on a chair with my back at them, as I tried to find a way of sneaking a banknote out of the pack. As I was minutely scrutinizing the make-up of the money pack and the way the security strips held them together, the thought of ever successfully slipping a banknote out without leaving a trace seemed a far-fetched fantasy. Still, deep down inside, I was convinced that there was a way. I only had to get around to finding it! I sat there still as if my body had frozen, while my mind was feverishly looking for a solution. When I had eventually worked it out, I shuddered with the shock of the revelation. My mom noticed the spasm and joked:

"There, there, Gheorghita! Is that stack of money burning your fingers?"

"Ha-ha!" I pretended to take up on Mom's joke. "I hope not, I'm trying to make friends with it and get to the bottom of the secret of money-making! Once found out, never forgotten! You can have it back now!" I said handing over the stack of money.

The last thing I wanted was to stir suspicion. Maria could see I was up to something, but she couldn't quite put her finger on it. The next day, Mom and I went to the bank and safely placed the money into an account. But when we returned home that evening, I was determined to practice my idea as much as I could. I had a 3-rubble banknote which I used as a template to produce a whole stack of papers of the same size. I also made two security strips, each of them two centimeters wide and I tied them one on the length and the other on the width of the pack, sewing the ends to make it as tight as possible. By the end of it, my stack of fake notes resembled like for like to the real thing.

For the next three days I was busy practicing getting out a banknote without leaving any traces behind. No matter what I did, nothing quite worked: when I left the security strips untouched, I managed to rip the banknote, and when I managed to save the banknote, I ruined the security strips. It all seemed a futile exercise, until I accidentally stumbled over a pair of pincers which my sisters left around. I also picked up a matchstick and split it halfway through. Equipped with such sophisticated tools which took my efforts to a whole new level, I set out to do the job: I clasped the corner of a banknote between the split ends of my matchstick, and then gently span it around the stick, while carefully pushing in the corners which stuck out now and again. After a few minutes of cautious delicate labor, ta-dah!!! Victory was mine: I managed to get out a whole banknote without ruining the security strips at all! My mind was already working in overdrive: I could just see the huge profit coming out of it!

Words can't describe my anxious wait until the next payment day when Mom brought home her payment. Circling around her like a sly fox, I pleaded with her to let me have the sealed stack for a few minutes.

"What's gotten into you, child! You've asked me for the money pack last time, as well!"

Mom raised an eyebrow,

"Well, Mom, you know me better than anyone: I like money and I hope one day money and me are meant to be!" I played on words to wave off her suspicions. "I just need to feel their magic touch, that's all!"

"When you put it like that, it's not a bad idea!" Mom confirmed with a smile and gave me the sealed pack. "You know the drill: don't damage the security strips!"

"Don't worry, Mom, I won't!" I reassured her.

The dog started barking outside alerting us that the neighbor next-door was at the gate. Mom looked out of the window and got ready to go outside:

"Wait here, I won't be long!" she told me.

I was overjoyed; I couldn't have wished for a better distraction! I stuck a chair in the door to allow myself some time if somebody came in, and rushed over behind the stove where Dad usually slept. I had everything ready: the first few minutes I needed to get the first banknote out were the hardest. My hands were trembling uncontrollably, the sweat was gushing through all my pores and my head was spinning. I knew it wasn't a rehearsal!

But I kept it together and in ten minutes I managed to get out as many as three banknotes! I decided to stop there, otherwise the security strips might have become far too loose on the pack and raised the suspicions of the cashier. If anything came out, Mom would have never trusted me again, and I had great plans for a future profit! I already had three 3-ruble notes, which was a lot of money for a child my age.

Looking back, that is probably the very moment when my time as a scamming mastermind started ticking over. As a result, many years later I would find myself at odds with the law in many Western countries. More on the topic later on in my future books. There is a time for everything!

I hid the banknotes in a good place, before I returned the pack to Mom.

"Are you coming with me to the bank?" she asked me as always.

"Of course I'm coming!" I smiled.

Throughout the journey my heart thumped in my chest and big drops of sweat covered the back of my head. When we finally got to the bank, I nearly broke my neck stumbling over my own feet while climbing up the stairs and I almost cracked my skull open, banging my head on the door. My heavy conscience was playing me up!

"What's up with you, Gheorghita, are you not feeling well?" my mom began to be concerned.

As soon as we reached the front of the queue, Mom handed over the pack of money and the cashier checked briefly the security strips. The goods ticked all the boxes, so he dropped the money in a drawer and marked Mom's check book I was watching everything closely, barely breathing.

When it was all over, and Mom and I walked out of the bank unscathed, I could have screamed with joy and excitement! By a funny coincidence, a police car on patrol slowly passed us; my sense of victory melted down and I felt a hard knot in my throat.

It was the first time in my life when I mustered all the revolt and bitterness against the government and their policies who would expect a family of eight to survive on a meagre income! It was a topic often discussed in my family, but only at that point did I fully understand the injustice of the situation. That revelation might have been brought home to me by my need to find an excuse for my newly discovered entrepreneurial spirit, but I wasn't too bothered about that! All the anger I had gathered over many years when I witnessed the livestock we reared being slaughtered and sold away in the market so that we could survive, sufficed and helped justify my less than orthodox methods of making money.

I kept under the hat my new source of income, but it didn't take long for Maria to work out that something else was going on. Even to this day, I have no idea what gave me away; perhaps the amount or the high quality of the sweets I was buying for myself! Maria could tell that I could afford spending a lot more than I used to. She knew where I kept the pocket money which our parents gave us, just like I knew where she kept hers, and whilst I treated myself to all the luxury sweets that money could buy, my saving didn't go down a penny! After many a thorough investigation, Maria came to the conclusion that my source of income must have been totally independent from our parents' benevolence. Following her instincts and all the clues she could put together, she eventually found my secret stash of banknotes.

When I returned from the fields one day, after a long day's work in the blazing sun, Maria took me aside and showed me the banknotes, holding me to ransom to tell her the truth.

"If you don't tell me where you've got them from, I'll tell Mom that you've stolen the money!" she threatened me.

If there was anything that made me see red in front of my eyes that was blackmail. Besides, I knew what could happen if Mom found me out!

"You can keep it all to yourself! Now, clear off and leave me be!" I sneered at her.

I could tell by the flicker in her eyes that Maria was really tempted to take up on the deal, but at second thought she replied:

"No way, José! This is not your lucky day! No easy way out of this one, I'm afraid, little bro!" and she waved a menacing finger under my nose to show that she meant business.

The fact that I was ready to give up so easily the money she was holding in her hand, convinced her that, wherever that was coming from, there was more. The change in strategy meant long-term gain for her and she snatched the opportunity without batting an eyelid. She pretended to casually go and look for Mom, while my blood was seething. Caught short (yet again!), I had to concede; so, I grabbed her hand forcefully and said through my teeth:

"All right, have it your way! I'll tell you where the money comes from, but you'll have to promise that it stays between us! You, pain in the neck!"

"Pain in the neck? Pain in the neck! What a way to talk to your big sister!" Maria played offended. "I wouldn't push it if I were you, especially in your situation!"

"OK, OK, I'm sorry!" I backed off.

"Too late! I feel offended!" Maria teased me, then she drew closer and whispered: "So, tell me, will you be able to get hold of some more of these?"

"Yes, I would…" I mumbled annoyed at my own lack of vigilance.

We went to a quiet corner where nobody could hear us and I told her everything about the new and ingenious way I could make money. She didn't believe me until I gave her a demonstration of my skills. Completely enlightened to the idea of quick and easy money-making, Maria was not shy to negotiate a high stake of the profit for herself: she wanted 50% of whatever I was making!

As for myself, I carried on getting my income in that way until I left home to go to school in the neighboring town. Mom never realized, and neither did the bank cashier. Somebody must have got the wrong end of the stick somewhere along the line, but such as life…

Not long after graduating secondary school, Maria left home to get her qualification as a nurse. As you can easily imagine, I hardly knew what to do with myself: all of a sudden, I didn't have to put up with the bossy ways of an older sister, I needn't share my secrets or my money with anyone… it was heaven… to begin with!

Two weeks passed, and I started feeling lonely, nothing was the same without Maria around! I missed her so much, that I would have given up anything only to have her back. It is true what they say: we don't really appreciate what we've got until it's taken from us! It was the first time when it dawned on me how much I cared about my sister!

Maria came home for the Christmas holidays after four months; she left at the end of August and came back just in time for Christmas. I was looking forward to seeing her again, and when she arrived accompanied by another one of my sisters, Nadia, who studied in the same place, I ran into her arms and we held each other for a few minutes. We both wept tears of joy. Mom couldn't believe her eyes: she came over and embraced us both:

"I knew I'd see the day when all grudges would be forgotten about! Better later than never!" she said thankfully looking at heavens.

I took a few steps back and eyed Maria from head to toe; she had changed. The look in her eyes was not that of a child any more.

"How long will you be home for?" was my first question.

"Only for a week, on Christmas holiday!" she replied.

I picked up her luggage and followed her inside.

"Why haven't you come home before now?" I half told her off.

"The school took us harvesting in the fields!" she replied somewhat apologetic.

We spent a long time talking to each other on that occasion: I told her what home was like without her, and she told me what school in town was without me! During that Christmas holiday I followed my sister around like a little poodle; I was her shadow wherever she went, which led to me witnessing one of her discussions with Mom:

"Mom, can I please have a new track suit and some decent pumps for my PE lessons?" Maria pleaded.

"What about the one that I bought you in August, before you went off to school?" Mom asked while going about her business in the kitchen.

"That was a cheap track suit and it looked worn out after the first wash. Besides, I did all the field harvesting in it, and now it looks really scruffy and worn out!" Maria explained.

"Where is your payment for all that work in the fields?" Mom asked her.

"They haven't paid me yet!" Maria replied.

"Then you'll have to wait until they do!" Mom kept to the point.

"But that can be well beyond spring time, Mom! Don't forget that we are talking about the government paying the students, which is likely the last thing on their priority list!" Maria insisted.

But Mom was not going to be easily persuaded. She had, indeed, bought a cheap tracksuit for Maria at the beginning of the school year. Maria made the most of it, but, in fairness to her, she got what she paid for: the tracksuit looked shabby beyond repair and Maria was embarrassed to wear it any longer.

"How much is the track suit you'd like to buy?" Mom questioned her.

"96 rubbles…" Maria said hesitantly.

"96 rubbles?" Mom almost had a fit and dropped the plate she was holding. "There is no way I can give you that sort of money! I'll borrow some money to pay for your travel expenses to school, but that's about it! Remember that it's not only you, I've got Nadia and Iulia to take care of, as well!"

Defeated, Maria started to cry.

The main expenditure for my big sisters was travelling back and forth to school and clothing. Food was never an issue, since Mom would pack up food and regularly send it to them.

"Please, Mom, I feel so embarrassed when my colleagues laugh at me!" Maria sobbed.

"Maria, that's the end of it! I don't want to hear another word!" Mom told her off.

Given the right circumstances, Mom would have gladly accommodated Maria's needs, but she had to consider everybody's needs.

"Look, it's not that bad! We've got a pregnant cow which is giving birth in three months' time; if you wait a bit, I can buy you a track suit then!" she said appealingly.

On hearing Mom's argument, I decided I had to do something about it: whether it was my love for my sister, or the ruthless idea of selling off the newly born calf, whose arrival I was looking forward to, or maybe a bit of both! Whatever the reason which triggered my reaction, I went into my secret stash, put everything together and counted it up. It mounted to a total of 125 rubbles.

I waited until my sister finished talking to Mom, and then I cut in front of her and took her aside. When we were safely tucked away from prying eyes, I produced the stash of banknotes and showed it to her:

"There you go, you can have it all. It's 125 rubbles, enough for a track suit and a pair of good pumps!" I told her handing over the money.

Maria's teary eyes widened up:

"What about you? Aren't you keeping anything behind?"

"What do I need money for?" I replied. "I've got enough clothes, I've got food in my belly and a roof over my head! You need it more than I do!"

Maria pulled me to her and gave me the biggest, warmest hug ever:

"I'll give it back to you, Gheorghita, I will! As soon as I get paid!"

"Oh, let's just forget about it!"

"Why won't you have it back?" she looked surprised.

"Because that's what family is for: to help each other in times of need!"

"Oh, brother, brother… Thank you so much! Are you sure about this?"

I gave her a hug and that helped her calm down. From then on, I helped Maria out with money until I left home myself. At the end of secondary school, I went off to a college in the same town where Nadia and Maria were studying.

As time passed, we saw a lot less of one another. I often thought to myself how much growing up and growing old can change people, but there is no way around it. Although we all chips off the old block, each had to go their own way and find their own path in life.

The nature of my relationship with Maria changed, as well, and I'm happy to say it was all for better. One occasion stuck in my mind: it was the anniversary of our village and all family gathered home to celebrate.

When I entered the house my eye was instantly drawn to a pair of denim trousers resting on the back of a chair. Back in those days, denim items were an expensive and rare commodity. I liked them so much, that I put them on without asking who they belonged to. They fit me perfectly.

"Whoever bought these for me, has a good eye!" I told the others jokingly.

When Maria entered the room and saw me sporting her trousers with such aplomb, she smiled and said quickly:

"It was a surprise present for you, but I see it didn't stay a secret for long!"

I jumped with joy and I paraded my new denims in front of the others for the rest of the evening. Only later on I was going to find out that Maria had bought the trousers for herself, but she couldn't bring herself to tell me and spoil my joy. She had managed to put the money together by doing harvesting work in the fields. It was her wages for four months of work: 100 rubbles. That was almost as much as Dad's monthly income, and usually an exorbitant price to pay for anything. Maria had planned on wearing them that evening at the disco.

I was so proud of my new denims, that I couldn't help myself taking them to school. During school-time, however, I had to change into my uniform according to the rules. I left my denim trousers in my lockers, but couldn't find them anywhere when I came back! Somebody must have spotted them and stole them from the lockers during lessons. My upset only grew greater thinking of what Maria would say when she found out about it!

Determined to make it up to her, I joined the older boys in the school when they went to help unload raw materials from freight trains. The money was good and I soon had enough to buy an identical pair of denims from a private trader, since that type of merchandise was not available in the shops.

I looked after them much better this time around, and I gave them to Maria for safe-keeping. In fact, we both agreed to take turns wearing them. Maria never found out what had happened to the pair which she had bought.

Slowly, Maria and I grew founder of each other and our relationship matured into a warm, genuine friendship. Maria apologized on a few occasions for having played so many pranks on me.

"You should be anything but sorry, big sis!" I would reply to her laughingly. "If we didn't have our pranks to remind us of our childhood, what would we be talking and laughing about now? Life is to be enjoyed, and if nothing else, we both turned out smarter than the average bear out of it all!"

CPSIA information can be obtained
at www.ICGtesting.com
Printed in the USA
LVHW082043160919
631219LV00012B/595/P